D1282929

THE TECHNIQUE
of
EDITING 16 mm. FILMS

THE LIBRARY
OF COMMUNICATION TECHNIQUES

THE TECHNIQUE OF
EDITING 16mm. FILMS

By
JOHN BURDER

Second Edition

COMMUNICATION ARTS BOOKS
Hastings House, Publishers
New York N.Y. 10016

© FOC___ ____ ____ MITED 1971

ISBN 0–8038–7114–7

First published 1958
Second Impression 1970
Second Edition 1971
Fourth Impression 1972

Library of Congress Catalog Card No. 67–31556

Printed and bound in Great Britain by
Billing & Sons Limited
Guildford and London

CONTENTS

5

FOREWORD

I have tried in these pages to outline the basic technical knowledge which I consider necessary before attempting to edit a film. I feel that my comments will be of particular interest to young professionals, film units in industry, and advanced amateurs.

I am indebted to Miss V. Bailey who has worked round the clock to translate the mysteries of my writing. My mother, for her untiring interest in all my film projects also wins my admiration, as do my film production colleagues, Alistair Cameron and Michael Nelson, both of whom have never failed to give me encouragement when I have been half-buried in typing paper!

I also wish to thank Mr. Alexis Svigoon who kindly read the proofs and pointed out many differences in British and American terminology, inserting U.S. terms wherever necessary.

Making a film is, in my opinion, a very practical art. Although much can be learned only by practice, I hope this book will provide a sound basis for practical exploration.

JOHN BURDER

1

THE PRODUCTION BACKGROUND

EDITING is one of the most important operations in making a film A film which has been well shot and brilliantly directed will be a total waste if put together badly. On the other hand, a film which has been shot well but without any particular distinction, can sometimes be very much improved by skilful editing. The editor aims to give the film a definite pace. He ensures that each scene is of the right duration, follows the preceding one smoothly and changes at the right point. He decides how long every shot remains on the screen. The good film editor combines artistry and technique so that the finished film flows from beginning to end without interruption or unevenness of any kind. He must maintain the interest of the audience throughout the film.

An editor has to prepare a detailed soundtrack, containing not only dialogue but music and effects, and he is responsible for the progress of the film from the time the processed camera originals are printed to the time the final edited version of the film is shown to the first audience.

If an editor is to produce a well-edited film he must first of all be presented with suitable raw materials to work with. So the film must be planned, scripted and photographed in such a way that it can be put together satisfactory. Continuity errors should be avoided and the right pictures must be photographed from the right angles. If the editor is to be presented with these materials and make something of them, his needs must be considered from the very first stages of pre-production planning.

Film Gauge

The editor should know from the outset which film gauge has been chosen for the production. He needs the right equipment and

9

experience to handle this gauge properly, before accepting the job. This applies especially to those working independently.

There are four formats to choose from: 35 mm., 16 mm., 8 mm. and Super 8 mm. The 35 mm. film is widest with 16 pictures in every foot of film. The 16 mm. pictures are smaller, with 40 pictures per foot. There are two kinds of 8 mm. film: the obsolescent standard 8, and the newer Super 8, which has a larger picture area.

Before the war 35 mm. was the only gauge used by professional film makers. The 16 mm. size was dismissed as "spaghetti" and 8 mm. was almost unheard of. Today, television makes spaghetti its staple diet, and professionals can work on both 35 mm. and 16 mm. with confidence. Television test transmissions have been carried out using 8 mm. film and we may well find that 8 mm. too will become a professional gauge. At present, to most professionals, 8 mm. is useful only as bootlaces.

The producer's choice of gauge depends on a number of factors not necessarily connected with the editor's task. These certainly override any feelings he may have about working with one gauge or another. The 35 mm. size is undoubtedly the most pleasant for him to work with. The pictures are easy to see and the film itself is comparatively easy to handle. But the producer is concerned with other aspects. Picture definition is noticeably better than on 16 mm. and the increased area available for soundtrack on release prints also makes better quality possible. A main disadvantage however is the cost of 35 mm. production. With sixteen frames (the name given to pictures) to every foot of 35 mm. film, and a thousand feet to every ten-minute roll, stock costs and processing charges are considerably higher than on 16 mm. Four hundred feet of 16 mm. will run for ten minutes, and that in itself means quite a reduction in expenditure. Most 35 mm. equipment is also rather heavy. The 35 mm. addict will say that it is better to carry heavy equipment than to rely on the picture quality of 16 mm. But nowadays this argument is rather a poor one. Much research and development has gone into the production and processing of 16 mm. materials. The variety of film stocks now available all over the world offers a very reasonable choice for every kind of work. If 16 mm. is projected on a very large screen it will never look as good as 35 mm., but many kinds of film production are not intended for big screen showings.

The relative cheapness of 8 mm. does not make up for serious disadvantages in other directions. While practically all the services, equipment and facilities available to the 35 mm. producer are also available to the man who shoots on 16 mm., this is still not the case on 8 mm. The range of camera equipment suitable for professional use is still very small and only a very limited range of film stocks can be obtained.

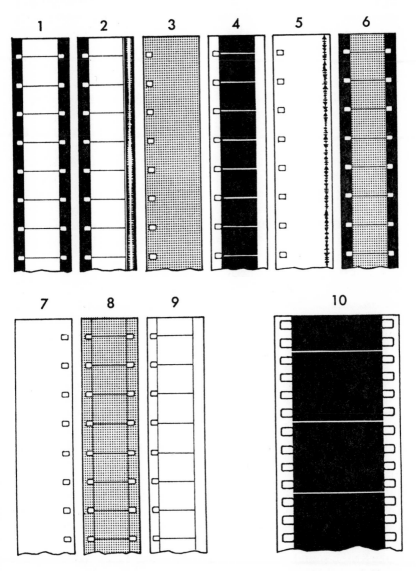

Types of film stock. 1, 16 mm. mute positive. 2, 16 mm. combined positive. 3, 16 mm. magnetic. 4, 16 mm. mute negative. 5, 16 mm. optical sound negative. 6, 16 mm. colour master. 7, 16 mm. white spacing. 8, 16 mm. colour negative. 9, 16 mm. colour positive. 10, 35 mm. mute.

When Super 8 mm. film was introduced, film stock and equipment manufacturers gradually decided to discontinue standard 8 mm. film and machines. By redesigning the 8 mm. film format and changing the shape of the perforations, the picture area had been considerably increased. Yet this Super 8 mm. film is still not in general professional use. Of course there was a time when 16 mm. was looked upon as an amateur sub-standard gauge, totally unsuitable for professionals! Today, it is more widely used than 35 mm., so the future of Super 8 should not be lightly dismissed. Manufacturers of editing equipment are beginning to show an interest in the professional possibilities of the new format but there are still some formidable technical drawbacks to the full adoption of this format professionally.

In the normal course of professional film production a special print is made for editing purposes. This print is made from the material actually exposed in the camera and is, in fact, a complete copy of what the camera records. When this print has been edited, the camera original is matched to it. This is done by matching small numbers which are to be found on the extreme edge of the film stock.

When the original has been matched to the cutting print, further prints can be produced from it. These prints will be of the edited version, and as they are produced from the original will be entirely free of the scratches and dirt collected on the editing print in the course of editing.

On 8 mm., however, you are immediately faced with two problems. The edge numbers (which are often known as key numbers) are not usually found on 8 mm. stock, so the matching of cutting print to camera original is a difficult task. It is also rather hard to find a laboratory able to produce good quality prints from strips of 8 mm. film.

No one really enjoys working with any kind of 8 mm. The pictures are difficult to see without projecting them on a screen and the film is also fragile to handle. Sound is also a problem, for here again there is no internationally accepted standard procedure. Some countries shoot their 8 mm. sound films at 24 frames per second, which is the standard sound running speed for the other two gauges. Others shoot at 18 frames per second. Some countries make 8 mm. sound prints with magnetic soundtracks and others use photographic ones.

Although 8 mm. and Super 8 are cheaper, they are clearly too restricted in scope for most professional requirements.

Interchanging Formats

A film shot on 35 mm. need not only be shown on 35 mm. It is quite possible to make 16 mm. prints from 35 mm. originals. In fact most 35 mm. feature films are reduced to 16 mm. for showing on ships, in aircraft and in a number of other special situations. The prints are made by a process known as reduction printing. Film shot on 35 mm. negative can be reduction printed straight on to a 16 mm. positive stock, although this method is not really recommended if several prints are required. Where several prints are needed it is far better to print your 35 mm. negative on a 35 mm. positive stock which has fine grain. The fine grain 35 mm. print can then itself be reduction printed on to 16 mm. negative, which can then be used for the direct production of 16 mm. copies. The exact method of making reduction prints is described in a later chapter.

The direct reduction of 35 mm. picture to 16 mm. can be quite satisfactory, but when making a number of copies, it is advisable to use a 16 mm. negative by the process just described. This 16 mm.

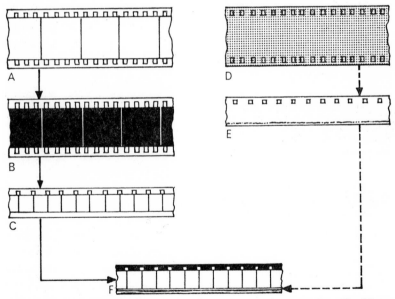

Making 16 mm. combined reduction prints from 35 mm. colour negatives. The 35 mm. colour negative (A) is printed on 35 mm. colour inter-positive (B) from which a 16 mm. reduction inter-negative (C) is made. The 35 mm. master magnetic (D) is re-recorded on 16 mm. optical sound negative (E) which is printed with (C) on 16 mm. colour positive (F).

13

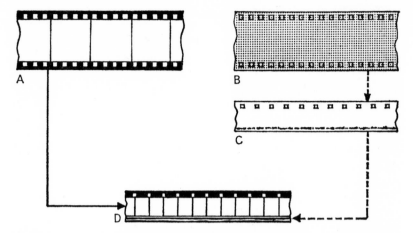

16 mm. married reduction prints from 35 mm. negative. The 35 mm. negative (A) is reduction printed with a re-recorded 16 mm. optical sound negative (C) on 16 mm. positive stock (D). The 16 mm. optical sound negative is made by re-recording from the 35 mm. master magnetic (B).

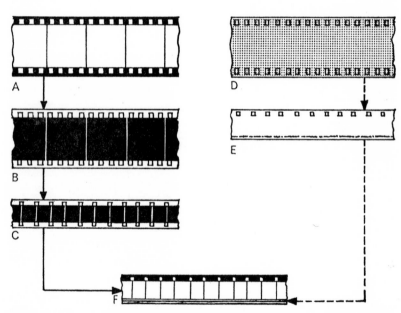

Making a number of 16 mm. married prints from 35 mm. negative. The 35 mm. negative (A) is printed on 35 mm. fine grain positive (B) which is itself printed on to 16 mm. reduction dupe-negative (C). The 35 mm. master magnetic (D) is simultaneously re-recorded on 16 mm. optical sound negative (E). The two 16 mm. negatives (C) and (E) are then printed together on 16 mm. positive stock (F).

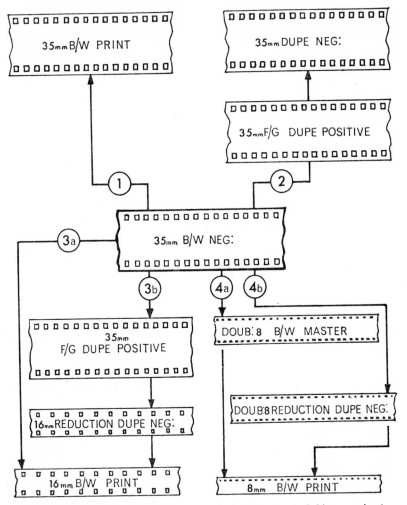

What you can make from a 35 mm. black-and-white negative incl. 16 mm. reductions.

negative is known as a 16 mm. reduction dupe-negative in the case of a black and white production, and an inter-negative where the film is in colour. The term "dupe" simply means duplicate and will be encountered at many stages of production.

There is another drawback to the production of direct reduction prints—that is, without making a 16 mm. negative. If the finished film runs for more than thirty minutes, which is the maximum amount of film many 35 mm. printing machines can accommodate, the 16 mm. print will have to have a splice in it. A 16 mm. negative, however, can be joined up. Most 16 mm. printing machines will accommodate thirty minutes of film, and many up to an hour. The 16 mm. print will then be free of splices.

The reduction printing of 35 mm. sound film is not really satisfactory and should be avoided whenever possible. It is preferable

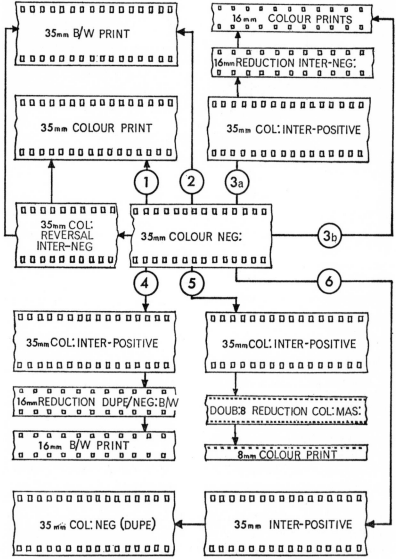

What you can make from a 35 mm. colour negative incl. 16 mm. reductions.

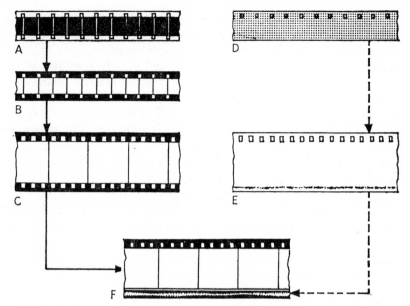

Making a 35 mm. blow-up print from 16 mm. negative. The 16 mm. negative (A) is printed on 16 mm. fine grain dupe positive (B) and re-exposed on 35 mm. negative (C). The 16 mm. master magnetic (D) is re-recorded on 35 mm. optical sound negative (E), which is printed, with (C) together on 35 mm. positive stock (F).

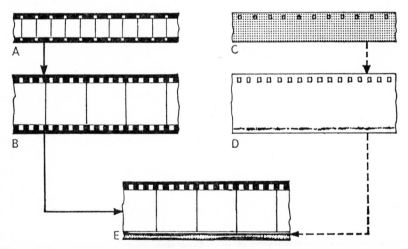

Making a 35 mm. blow-up print from 16 mm. colour master. The 16 mm. colour master (A) is blown up to 35 mm. inter-negative (B) whilst the 16 mm. master magnetic (C) is re-recorded as 35 mm. optical sound negative (D). Both (B) and (D) are then printed together on 35 mm. colour positive (E).

to start again with the master magnetic recording and have it re-recorded on a suitable 16 mm. negative sound stock. This should be done if the picture is being printed from 35 mm. negative or from an intermediate 16 mm. dupe. Sound and picture negatives must be put in synchronisation in the way described later in this book.

As we have seen, a film shot on 35 mm. can be used to produce 35 mm. and 16 mm. prints without difficulty. Those working on 16 mm. should concentrate on 16 mm. prints for, although it is perfectly possible to blow 16 mm. up to 35 mm., this rarely provides good quality. There have nevertheless been some notable exceptions to this general rule. A recent film on the possible effects of a nuclear war was extremely well photographed on 16 mm. Its success on television prompted the producers into making 35 mm. prints for cinema showing. They reversed the reduction printing process and loaded a laboratory printer with a 16 mm. fine grain positive (printed from the 16 mm. negative) and a roll of unexposed 35 mm. negative. The 16 mm. print was then re-exposed on the 35 mm.

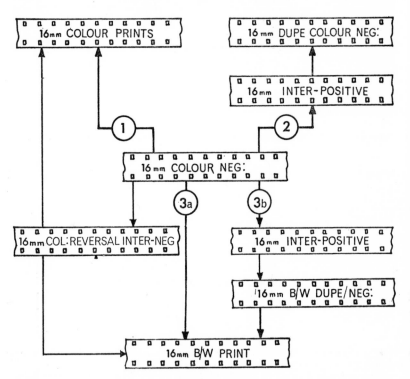

What you can make from a 16 mm. colour negative also double eight colour film.

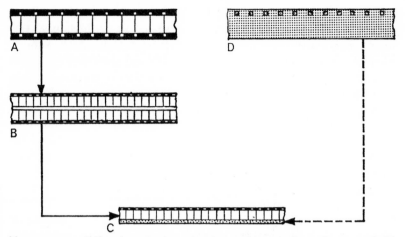

16 mm. masters (A) can be reduction printed on to 8 mm. or Super 8 mm. stock (B). Two copies are printed side by side on stock 16 mm. wide with 8 mm. perforations. After printing, the film is split to 8 mm. (C) and magnetically striped. The master magnetic sound (D) can then be re-recorded on the stripe.

negative and a "blow-up dupe-neg" was thus produced for 35 mm. printing. The resulting increase in grain size and the slight loss in definition could be excused in view of the nature of the subject of the film: nuclear war. Indeed, many of the scenes of panic and destruction were considerably improved by the rather "newsreely" appearance of some of the material.

Both 35 mm. and 16 mm. can be satisfactorily reduced to standard 8 mm. and Super 8 mm. Most laboratories can print 35 mm. and 16 mm. originals on to 8 mm. but few are able to make single prints. Most printing stocks are supplied in 16 mm. size with 8 mm. or Super 8 mm. perforations and laboratories thus print two copies simultaneously on opposite sides of the same piece of film. When the prints are processed, the film is split to 8 mm. or Super 8 mm. size.

Negative and Reversal Film

Now let us consider the material itself and examine the main differences between negative and reversal stocks. Exposed negative, when processed, produces an image where black appears as white and vice-versa. When the negative is reproduced by printing on a suitable positive stock, the image will appear correct with shadow

19

areas again appearing as black and highlights as white. On a reversal stock the negative image is reversed in processing so that tone values on the film are similar to those in the original subject. This is carried out on one piece of film and does not involve a separate negative intermediate stage. The reversal image is, in fact, a positive image just like an ordinary photographic print taken from a negative.

A film can be photographed on either reversal or negative material. The editor arranges for prints to be produced from the film exposed in the camera. Negative camera stocks are printed on positive stocks and reversal materials are duplicated on other reversal materials. Either way, the editor receives a positive working copy. The actual stock used in the camera is the camera master or original. It must never be projected, be it negative or reversal. It has only to be scratched or torn and the damage is irreparable and will be part of the film for ever. The master must be carefully guarded from the moment it is first taken out of its can and loaded in the camera, to the time it comes to the editor from the processing laboratory, and ever after.

When the film has been exposed in the camera it is sent to a laboratory for processing. The editor asks the laboratory to supply a print for editing. This is a cutting copy or work print. The laboratory then prints the processed negative on to a positive stock, or duplicates the original reversal exposures on a reversal stock, and sends the editor the print and the original. The print will be used for editing. The original remains uncut until the final edited version of the film is approved. It is only at this stage that the edited cutting copy is passed to a technician known as a negative cutter who, working with immense care, matches the master to it, cut for cut and scene for scene. He does this by referring to numbers printed on the edge of the original material and duplicated on the edge of the cutting copy. These numbers are known as key or edge numbers. You will find one number in every foot of film.

After matching, the master material is returned to the laboratory. A new print of the edited film is made from it. This is free from the splices or scratches which by this time have accumulated on the cutting copy. Now the laboratory simply loads a film-printing machine with the edited master material and a new unexposed reel of positive stock and exposes the original on the new stock. After development the new print is ready for use.

Sometimes, for insurance or safety reasons the uncut master is copied and stored in case anything happens to the actual master itself. This duplication is also undertaken when the master has been matched to the edited cutting copy. Although duplicates lack the impeccable quality of an original they also lack the splices always found in an edited original.

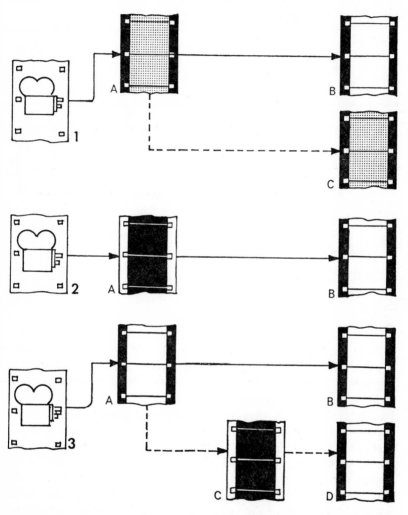

Production of cutting copy from originals. 1, From colour master: reversal processed (A); duplicated on black-and-white reversal stock (B); or duplicated on colour reversal (C). 2, From black-and-white negative (A) contact printed on black-and-white positive (B). 3, From black-and-white reversal: reversal processed (A); duplicated on black-and-white reversal (B); or printed on negative stock (C) which, when processed, can be printed on positive (D).

21

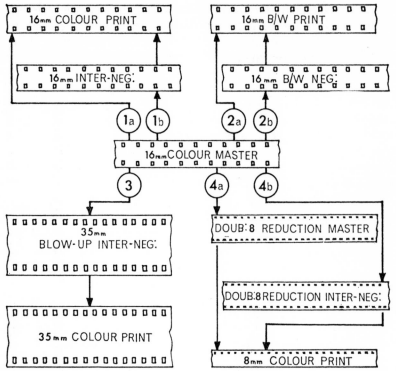

What you can make from a 16 mm. colour master incl. 35 mm. and 8 mm. derivatives

Colour Reversal

The term 'master' is a very wide one. Up to this point I have used it to describe all materials exposed in the camera, both negative and reversal. When working with 16 mm. colour you can shoot on either a colour negative film, like Eastmancolor, or a reversal stock, like Ektachrome. A reversal colour original when exposed and processed is known as a colour master. It can be duplicated in the same manner as a black and white reversal, on monochrome reversal stock, to provide a black and white print for editing purposes. If a colour cutting print is required, it can be duplicated on a colour reversal material. When editing has been completed, the colour master is matched to the cutting copy and the cut colour master can then be duplicated on a colour reversal stock. If, however, a number of 16 mm. colour prints are required it is quite a good idea to produce a negative from the edited colour master. A laboratory can do this. They simply print your colour master on a special 16

22

mm. negative stock designed for printing purposes and not for use in the camera. The negative can then be used for making further prints. Wear and tear on the edited camera master is reduced by using the new unspliced negative to make all further prints. Such a negative, produced by the laboratory, is known as an inter-negative.

Original colour negative can also be copied. If you only want a few prints of a final edited film, it is quite possible to print a cut original colour negative on colour positive stock. This is all very well for producing a few copies, but if you expect to make more than five, a duplicate colour negative should be produced to avoid wearing out the original. There are two ways of making a duplicate colour negative. The original cut negative can be printed on an

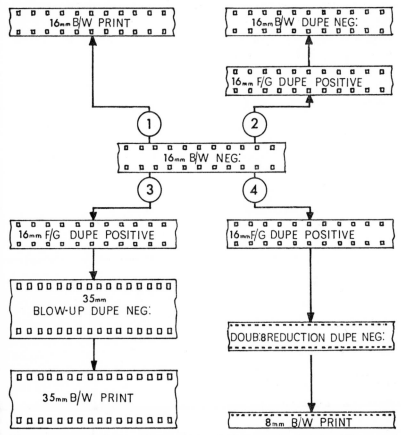

What you can make from a 16 mm. black-and-white negative including 35 mm. and 8 mm. black-and-white derivatives.

intermediate positive stock. The inter-pos can then be re-exposed in the laboratory on a new negative stock, which can itself be used for the production of further prints. In the course of this operation, picture and colour quality can sometimes suffer though, if the original is of good quality, the loss should only be marginal. The alternative is to use a new film stock recently introduced: reversal internegative.

Reversal internegative stock is made by Kodak, for laboratory use. It is a special stock which enables a duplicate colour negative to be made from an Eastmancolor original negative in one direct stage. There is no need for an intermediate positive. Laboratories can print original colour negative on reversal internegative stock and the new reversal interneg., when processed, can be printed on colour positive in exactly the same way as a colour negative original. All the loss of definition, caused by making an intermediate positive, can be avoided. So it is an excellent innovation, and ideal for making the duplicate negatives needed to produce release prints.

Working with Reversal

When a reversal master is exposed in the camera, you have, from

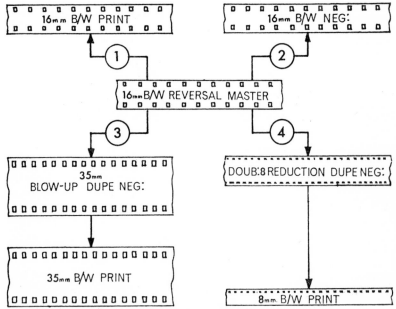

What you can make from a 16 mm. black-and-white reversal master including 35 mm. and 8 mm. derivatives.

the start, a positive image. A reversal master can be duplicated on other reversal stock thus producing another positive copy. This is the ideal way of producing a small number of prints. But printing reversal on reversal is usually more expensive than printing negative on positive so, if a number of copies are required, it may be worth making a negative from a reversal original. The negative can then be used for making release prints. The master will be saved wear and tear, and you may save additional expense.

If a film being shot might possibly form the basis of several productions, reversal stocks are worth serious consideration. If, for example, the film shows scenes of the building of a ship and the plan is to use some of the scenes immediately in a film about the company who will operate the ship, and then later use the same scenes again in a different way in another film about the ship herself, reversal stock would be the best to use. If a film is shot on reversal film the editor can arrange for a negative to be produced from the uncut reversal. This negative can be printed and when editing is complete on the first film, the negative can be matched to the cutting copy without touching the reversal original. Where only a few copies are needed you can use reversal material. In other cases it is better to use negative positive procedure for making prints or shoot on reversal and make a negative for printing.

2

SOUND IN PRODUCTION

THE editor is concerned with one other important pre-production decision: the choice of sound system to be employed. On the finished film there are two different kinds of soundtrack to choose from. They are magnetic soundtracks, and optical ones. What are the advantages and disadvantages of each of these types of soundtrack and when should each type be used?

Optical Sound

For release prints, which is simply another way of saying for prints produced for general showing and not for use in the course of film production, an optical soundtrack is almost standard. An optical soundtrack is one which is printed photographically on the side of the film alongside the picture. For 16 mm. film the actual frame area of one frame of film is 7·47 mm. high and 10·41 mm. across (in the camera gate) and the soundtrack of an optical track on 16 mm. film has a full width of 0·085" or 2·15 mm., though the projector only reads part of this area and the signal is contained within an area of about 1·8 mm. An optical soundtrack is printed alongside the film by the laboratory. They can print an optical track from a negative or duplicate it from a reversal sound master track. The editor must, however, first of all synchronise the optical soundtrack with the edited master picture material so the two can be printed together in synchronism on the positive stock. How this is done is described in detail in the explanation of the process of negative cutting. Most 16 mm. sound projectors can show a film with an optical soundtrack.

Magnetic Sound

The editor will also be concerned with magnetic soundtracks. Basically there are two kinds of magnetic sound: separate magnetic and combined, which is often known as sound stripe. Let us consider first the uses and advantages of sound stripe.

Stripe, as the name suggests, is again a soundtrack located on the edge of the picture. On 16 mm. film magnetic stripe can be placed in the same area as the optical soundtrack to offer an alternative. Or, a narrow magnetic stripe can be placed alongside, clear of the actual optical recording. Magnetically striped films are easily recognised. The stripe itself is simply a coating of brown ferrous oxide applied to the film. The main difference is in the way the soundtrack is recorded and reproduced.

Optical soundtracks are printed from a negative or reversal master via a photographic process. Magnetic sound has to be re-recorded magnetically. You simply replay the master magnetic recording on one machine, and re-record the soundtrack magnetically on the stripe on the edge of the film, on another machine. Sound synchronisation here, too, must be preserved, as we shall see later. The audio quality of a magnetic recording is usually considerably better than an optical one. The background hiss characteristic of optical sound is very much reduced with magnetic and the range of sound obtainable is usually far greater.

Unfortunately there are quite a large number of projectors which cannot project 16 mm. magnetically striped prints. Optical tracks are reproduced by shining a light through the optical soundtrack on to a photo-electric cell and thus to an amplifier; magnetic stripes have to be replayed via a replay magnetic head. But these heads are not yet standard fittings on 16 mm. projectors.

Separate Soundtracks

Magnetic sound is undoubtedly preferable for good quality but, at present, it is wiser to produce an optical track for release prints. An editor will, however, use magnetic tracks throughout the main stages of editing, though the tracks he uses will be separate ones and not alongside the same piece of film as the visual image.

Separate magnetic tracks are an essential part of practical editing. If you're working on 16 mm. you will probably use 16 mm. magnetic tracks. In appearance they resemble the 16 mm. film exposed in the camera, being the same size. Like the camera stock, the magnetic film has perforations, though the perforations are only on one side and not both as with some camera film stocks. The soundtrack film is opaque, being entirely covered with ferrous oxide. Unlike the optical track, you cannot see a soundtrack on it. You need

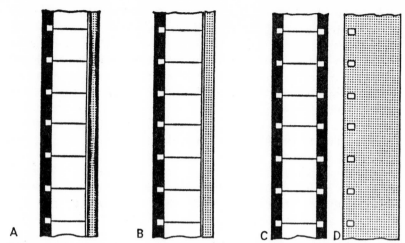

Different types of soundtrack. (A) Combined optical. (B) Combined magnetic (stripe); the signal is invisible. (C+D) Mute print with separate magnetic track.

equipment to hear it. For editing, however, it has many advantages. By far the most important of these is its high original quality, and relatively small loss of quality when it is re-recorded. In the course of making a film, soundtracks have to be re-recorded several times, as we shall see. Magnetic tracks lose a little quality in the course of these recording transfers. Optical tracks cannot be satisfactorily copied without a noticeable increase in background noise and distortion. The magnetic track is also easily spliced, and the join—provided you don't splice in the middle of sound, is inaudible. When you join an optical track, you will always hear a slight difference in quality when the splice passes through the projector.

The editor therefore makes use of separate magnetic soundtracks. He can edit them with his piece of action (the cutting copy) and will eventually mix all the separate magnetic soundtracks together in a sound dubbing theatre to make one master recording. His separate soundtracks may include tracks of dialogue, tracks of music and sound effects. These can all be mixed together to make the final master magnetic recording. This recording is then transferred to a magnetically striped print, or to an optical sound negative for printing.

Synchronised Sound

There are two main kinds of sound to consider; synchronised and unsynchronised. It is said to be synchronised when it exactly

28

matches the picture. In the case of someone speaking, the lip movement of the person speaking must exactly match the dialogue. The difference of even a frame will be noticeable. If sound and picture match exactly, the sound may be said to be synchronised or simply "in sync.". It is very easy to think of sync. sound only in terms of synchronised dialogue. This is misleading for, if the film editor does his job well, there will be many other places where synchronisation is obvious. Such places are known as sync. points. Every audible footstep, each blow of a hammer, every slam of a door and every strike of a match is a sync. point.

But not all sound is synchronised. Background noises and atmospheres need not be accurately synchronised and indeed dialogue spoken out of view of the camera need not be synchro-

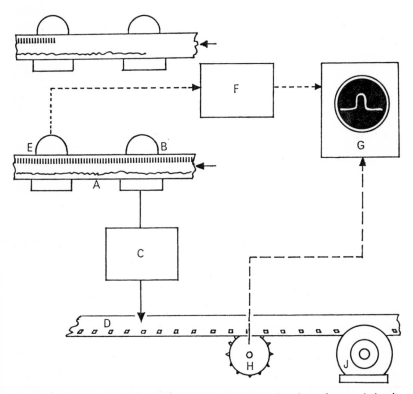

The sync. pulse recording system. Recorded sound is picked up from the tape A, by the head B, and fed through an amplifier C, to be re-recorded on the magnetic film D. The pulse is picked up by the head E, and fed through an amplifier F, to an oscilloscope G, where it is compared with another from the moving film H, and they are kept in step by altering the speed of the motor J.

nised either. Commentaries (narrations), for example, are not photographed in sync. They, and many other sounds used in the course of production are recorded "wild"—the term given to sound recorded independently of the cameras.

When a film is first planned, it must be decided whether or not synchronised dialogue is going to be used. If it is, then a camera and suitable recording equipment which can be interlocked (in synchronism) are needed. The normal way of preserving synchronism between a camera and recorder is by using a pulse which is recorded alongside the actual sound recording on the separate recorder. The same pulse is later used to interlock the recorder and another recording machine when copies of the original recording are needed for editing. An exact copy, running at the same speed is thus ensured.

There are two possible ways of shooting synchronised dialogue. Recordings of synchronised sound can be made either on a magnetic stripe, on the edge of the actual film in the camera. Or recordings can be made on a separate recorder locked to the camera by a synchronizing pulse. Recorders taking $\frac{1}{4}''$ tape are quite often used for this purpose. When the production company is deciding which of these systems to employ, it is worth their considering the advantages and disadvantages each system offers from an editor's point of view. With the striped film, sound and picture are already on the same piece of film. When the exposed material is taken out of the camera and sent for processing the magnetic stripe is processed with it. The processing in no way affects the magnetic stripe but the processed film can then be shown straight away as a combined magnetic sound print. If the sound has been recorded on separate $\frac{1}{4}''$ tape synchronised by pulse, this tape must first of all be transferred by a sound transfer studio to perforated magnetic film. While this is being done the camera master can be processed. The two pieces of film must then be synchronised by the editor. Now, if there is projection equipment capable of showing a silent picture with a separate piece of perforated magnetic film, you can show the sound and picture together. But in all probability there will not be a suitable projector. For normal use the magnetic sound must again be transferred, this time to optical. A new print combining the optical soundtrack and picture on the same piece of film must then be made. The use of a separate recording is therefore rather a longer process. Bearing these points in mind which is the right system to use?

The striped film has certain advantages if you are producing an

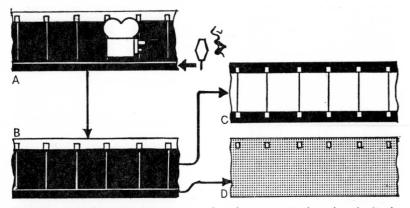

To make a striped sound print you can either shoot on striped stock and edit the processed master (A) or shoot mute (C) and print the picture mute and have it magnetically striped (B) whilst editing with a separate magnetic track (D) which can then be transferred to the striped picture.

on-the-spot news report where speed is essential to get the finished film on the screen. Simple sequences can be adequately edited using sound stripe and many television news reports use this technique. If however you want to undertake more advanced editing, the sound on the magnetic stripe will have to be transferred to separate magnetic film when the film has been processed. This will allow the editor more freedom. He can cut his picture at any point, and will not first of all have to consider the sound he is forced to cut simultaneously alongside the action. With a striped original, he has to cut sound and picture at the same point. With separate magnetic tracks he will have more freedom. He can carry sound on, and change the picture at a different point if he wishes. Separate sound-tracks are essential for creative editing. If sound has been recorded on separate $\frac{1}{4}''$ tape, locked by pulse, that too must be transferred to perforated magnetic film before editing. But that transfer can be done while the film is being processed. The tape should be sent to a suitable sound transfer studio, where it will be transferred to perforated magnetic film without loss of synchronisation. With the transfer and a print made from the processed camera original editing can begin.

As a rule, if a straight news-type interview is being produced where speed comes first, film which is itself magnetically striped may be the best thing to use. If it is a documentary, or a commercial, it is better to record either directly on to synchronised separate

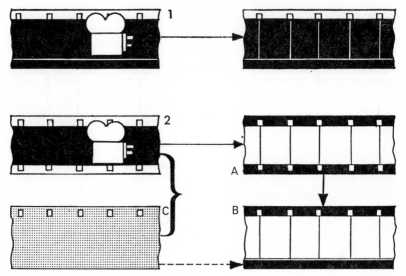

Ways of editing a striped sound recording. I, Shoot on magnetically striped stock making a simultaneous striped recording. You can edit the processed master. 2, Shoot on striped stock and transfer striped sound from processed master to separate magnetic and edit both, using picture as mute.

magnetic film, or on to tape which is properly synchronised to the camera. The tape can then itself be transferred to perforated magnetic film. All this applies in the case of shooting synchronised dialogue.

Unsynchronised Sound

If the film does not have to involve synchronised speech it is quite feasible to shoot it without a sound camera. There are a number of ways of adding sound in the course of editing.

A film can be edited silently, and, when the picture assembly has been finalised, a commentary can be added without music or sound effects. Or you can produce a full and detailed soundtrack of music, sound effects and commentary. This latter course is highly recommended. Too many films are thrown together with a few gramophone records added where there isn't any commentary. A good film editor will take immense care to find the right sound effects and use them to advantage to attract the attention of an audience and to maintain their interest. We shall see later how a detailed soundtrack is assembled. In the early stages of pre-production planning the first decision on the type of soundtrack must be made and the editor's advice is well worth obtaining. The producer must decide, before a film is photographed, if he wants a really detailed soundtrack. If so, editing would be very much easier if a sound recordist operating portable recording equipment which works independently of the camera accompanies the camera team. The tracks he records will be "wild tracks". They do not exactly match the film exposed in the camera, for recording and camera equipment are not locked in synchronism. Synchronised dialogue cannot be recorded in this manner, but background sound can. The editor will find these wild tracks very useful when he starts to build up his soundtrack.

An editor can probably obtain recordings of many basic sound effects from sound libraries. But the use of copyright recordings can be expensive and it is often difficult to find a suitable recording of good quality. I once spent a great deal of time trying to find a recording of the noise made by a car hoist moving a car along the production assembly line of a car factory. The search was completely fruitless. Eventually I found a recording of a household food mixer and played it at the wrong speed. It sounded exactly like the hoist I had been looking for!

Using Wild Tracks

The editor will find wild tracks exceedingly useful, but how exactly are they used in a film? Where there is dialogue they are used to fill in the background. And where there is no dialogue they must speak for themselves, drawing attention to the items of interest. Let us consider each of these uses. Imagine first of all a dialogue sequence filmed in a busy street. An interviewer is questioning passers by on some topic of interest. The script calls for the editor to intercut shots of the interviewer and the people who are being questioned. The shots are photographed as sync. takes, by a camera locked to a separate recorder using $\frac{1}{4}''$ tape. When the shooting has finished the camera master is processed and the editor arranges for the sound to be transferred to magnetic film. He then resynchronises the dialogue and the action and starts to cut the scenes together. Where he cuts the picture he also cuts the sound. When he listens to the finished result, however, he finds that the sound quality of the track differs considerably from interview to interview. The reason is obvious. The interviews were filmed in a busy street and the amount of traffic passing the interviewer differed considerably. In the early morning when the first interviews were photographed there were very few vehicles but by midday the streets were crowded. To improve the sound quality the editor uses a wild track in addition to the dialogue. In the course of filming, the sound recordist has also recorded a number of wild tracks of different traffic noises. The editor builds up suitable background noise tracks in addition to his other track of dialogue. When editing is completed he mixes the soundtracks together in a dubbing theatre and thus smoothes out the differences in background noise.

Combining Wild Tracks

An alternative use of wild tracks is where the film has been photographed without synchronised dialogue, or indeed synchronised sound of any kind. Again, take a street scene example. This time the film shows general activity in a central city street. The editor looks carefully at the cameraman's picture. What exactly does it show? There are a number of cars and commercial vehicles in the street, all moving slowly. One car appears to have broken down on the far side of the street and several others are held up behind it. There's also a bus stop and a bus draws up and stays there long enough for passengers to get off and on. The bus then moves off again, and at that point the cameraman has ended the shot. What sounds will the editor need to bring this picture to life? He could leave it silent and just put commentary over it, but it would appear dead. Far better to recreate the sounds of the original scene. To do that he will need suitable raw material in the form of wild tracks. First of all he will need a general traffic roar of slow-moving traffic as a background. He will also need the sound of a bus stopping and starting. These are basic necessities. If he wants to do the job well he will then add some detail. On the far side of the street motorists are being held up behind the car which has broken down. A few impatient motor horns will liven up proceedings but should not be overdone. When the bus stops and people get off a little brake squeal from the bus would not be out of place and a bell could be heard before the driver moves off. If people can be seen on any pavements a background murmur of conversation would also be in order. All these are small points, and some of them should not be overplayed, but they do add detail. And in a soundtrack, detail means life.

Some of the sounds I have listed can be satisfactorily obtained from sound libraries. Motor horns and brake squeal are easy effects to find. The two traffic backgrounds, of general road and bus stopping and moving off would be very much better recorded at the time of filming, by a recordist. These would be wild tracks. They are raw materials the editor needs and provision for obtaining them must be considered in the early stages of pre-production planning.

Wild tracks should be recorded wherever possible, especially where background sounds are needed. Don't think that because a scene is being photographed as a synchronised take wild tracks will not be needed. They will probably be wanted just the same. This is particularly true where background noise has been deliberately cut out in the course of synchronised shooting. This often happens when using a chest microphone for an interview so that the voices of the speakers can be heard without being drowned by background noise.

If two people are seen talking on the floor of a factory, the sound recordist shooting the actual sync. dialogue may find the background clatter of the factory blots out the conversation. To overcome this he may give the speakers chest microphones, designed to pick up only the voices of the people who are speaking, and not the factory noise in the background. These sync. speeches will be recorded on a recorder locked in sync. with the camera, or on a camera built to record on magnetically striped stock. When the film is assembled, the vast factory scene will appear deceptively silent if the two voices recorded are the only sounds heard. For this reason, wild tracks of the sounds of the factory must be recorded in the course of filming. The recordist should wait until the dialogue sequences have been completed, and then record a few minutes of background. This enables the editor to re-unite background and dialogue by mixing the two soundtracks together. As the two sounds are recorded separately he can ensure that the level of each recording is correct. In the final mixed soundtrack, dialogue will stand out clearly above an audible but not deafening background.

Sound for Editing

For interiors and exteriors, then, arrangements should always be made for someone to record wild tracks. This is particularly important when there is no sync. dialogue, for if the scene is left mute, or just held under commentary, it will lose much of its life. In the factory scene just mentioned, if commentary alone were heard over the picture, the noise and bustle of the factory would disappear and an audience may well lose interest. The film would assume the style of an old instructional film for schools where background effects were sometimes left out for reasons of economy and for fear of distracting students from the wealth of information contained in the commentary.

If the editor is to produce an adequate soundtrack, he must have wild tracks to help him. Out of doors he will need traffic, or other atmosphere recordings and indoors too, natural sounds should be recorded wherever possible. The sounds used will then be authentic and interesting.

I am reminded of a film producer who did not record any wild tracks in the course of a film about agriculture in the main European countries. He relied on recordings supplied by one sound library. Unfortunately they were only able to supply one recorded effect for open field atmosphere. The producer used the effect every time he had a shot of an open field or countryside. It was a very distinctive recording—a lark and a few wood pigeons were exceedingly obvious and, in the finished film the same lark and wood pigeon appeared to follow the unit round most of the European countries. Had he taken the trouble to record two or three wild tracks, some variation could have been made.

Where wild tracks are used without synchronised dialogue, they are particularly important, and the editor may have to rely entirely on sound to give impact to the scene. Let us again look at the factory example. Perhaps, after the sync. dialogue sequence we have mentioned, the film goes on to show various machines in use on the factory floor. Wild tracks recorded in the course of filming will help the editor to recreate the atmosphere of the factory. But a general atmosphere is not really enough. It must contain detail. Recordings should be made of the sound of each machine portrayed in a separate shot. The editor will then use these recordings with a background track to build up a detailed soundtrack with some perspective. The use of sound in films, particularly in documentaries, is fascinatingly important and wild tracks have a vital part to play.

If one particular car plays an important part in a film, make sure that plenty of sound of it has been recorded wild. Tracks of the doors being opened and closed, engine starting and ticking over, engine revving, and the car pulling away are basic necessities. Tracks of the car passing at speed and slowly, together with interior noise when the car is in motion, including gear changes up and down should also be recorded. Recordings of any domestic doors opened and shut in the course of location filming are often useful too.

36

Recording Details

Details in sound are always important. Consider a sequence showing operations in one large general office. The sequence consists of one long shot showing the whole office. We can see people working on various machines in all parts of the office. We then cut to a series of closer shots showing some of the people who work here, ending with a shot of the man in charge picking up a telephone and speaking into it. In the course of filming, only the man's telephone conversation will be shot as a sync. take. The rest of the action will be shot mute and the editor will rely on wild tracks to recreate the atmosphere and the pace of work going on in the office. If only the minimum can be recorded it should be the general background of office rumble: the sort of noise you would expect to hear from the first camera position shooting the long shot. But it is not really adequate. There must be wild tracks of the machines people are working on in the closer shots. When all these are cut together by an editor who understands sound and pace, the effect should be satisfactory and interesting to an audience. The extra sounds will give depth to the pictures. In the last shot the ring of the telephone bell, and the sound of the telephone receiver being picked up should also be recorded wild, although these sounds could be obtained from a library disc if necessary. With clear sync. dialogue recordings and a variety of wild tracks, the editor will have suitable sound material to work with.

Identifying the Take

In the course of filming it is always important that the beginning or end of every exposure be clearly identified. The editor relies on this identification. This is especially so in a sync. take which should be properly identified in the accepted manner, using a clapper board in the case of separate sound recordings.

Before shooting a synchronised take the director first asks the sound recordist to start his equipment running. He then tells the cameraman to start the camera. When both camera and recorder are running at the right speed, the director calls out "Mark it!" Someone will then walk into shot in clear view of the camera, with clapper board. The board is simply a small blackboard on which the title of the film, the scene and take numbers and the cameraman's name are written. Possibly also the name of the production company and the director. The board itself is divided into two parts. The lower half is the larger, providing space for the writing

37

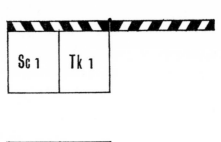

When identifying the start of a mute take, the clapper board should be held open. I↑
unable to identify the start of a take, hold the clapper upside down at the end of it,
banging it together if sound has been recorded.

and a small black and white striped bar is hinged to the top. The
man holding the board lifts this bar up and reads the writing written
on the lower section of the board. "Scene ten, take one." He then
bangs the two parts of the board together and moves quickly out
of view of the camera. The director shouts "action", and the
scripted shot gets under way. The clapper serves a very definite
purpose when sound is recorded on a separate tape or magnetic
film. Before the film can be edited, or indeed before the results of
the day's filming can be seen on a screen, sound and picture must
first be synchronised. Without the identification of sound and
action provided by the clapper the synchronisation of material is
a far more difficult task.

Sometimes part of a film may have been shot without a clapper
board. Perhaps someone forgot to take it or it was lost in transit.
This does not mean that the camera team cannot help the editor
synchronise his material. Someone can stand in front of the
camera near a microphone and clap his hands together. If the
editor can see the point where the hands meet and identify the clap
on the recorded track he will be helped considerably. If the scene
and take number can be written on something other than a clapper
board and held in shot, and be read aloud for the benefit of the
recording, this will help the editor considerably.

Sometimes with location work it is not possible to identify the start of a scene, particularly with on-the-spot events. But the clapper can then be used at the end of the shot—held upside down. The clapper board is used for all shots. Where there is no sound, the top part of the board is held open. The editor then knows that the take is mute and will not waste time looking for a soundtrack which has never been recorded.

Sometimes it is not possible to use a clapper board or even clap hands in front of the camera. The team may be filming a concert or some other scene where those taking part would be disturbed by a loud bang. They can still help the editor by marking synchronisation, although they may have difficulty speaking the scene and take number. A microphone can be held in front of the camera and tapped once clearly, with a finger. The editor is then able to find the point where the finger touches the microphone and identify it on the track. The noise heard by any spectators would not be objectionable.

3

VISUALS IN PRODUCTION

THE editor will rely completely on the material he receives from studio and location filming. Notes provided by the production secretary will do much to help him, and the watchful eyes of a director and production secretary can be very useful to an editor.

Continuity

During the production, the director and production secretary must pay particular attention to the question of continuity, for if scenes are to be edited together, they must be planned with this in mind from the initial script. The director and production secretary must both notice the exact position of all properties and actors at the end of each shot. So that they are able to match up the shot which follows. This is not important when the scene changes from a shot showing one thing or person, to something completely different. If, however, the same subject appears in two successive shots, smooth continuity is important. Attention to detail in the course of filming is vital if mistakes are not to be made.

Let us consider a number of examples. The script calls for shots of two people standing together in a café drinking. They are talking to each other and the sequence consists of shots of the two people together, intercut with close-ups of each of the people who are talking. In the first of the two shots the man on the left is listening and the one on the right is doing the talking. The one who listens holds a cup in his left hand. In his right hand he holds a spoon which he uses to stir the contents of the cup. He looks at the man who is talking to him. In the following shot the camera has been moved to concentrate on the man who is listening. In the course of the shot he begins to answer the man who has been talking. The two shots are filmed separately with a break in between. Since the last shot was completed the studio has been altered considerably.

An extra light has been set up to fill in some shadows on the second man's face, shadows which were not apparent from the first camera position. The camera has been moved and microphones are in different positions. When the actors return to the set for shooting the second shot, the man who is to be photographed is suddenly worried. He cannot remember if he was holding his tea cup with his left hand or his right. Had he started to stir the sugar? He cannot remember. Fortunately for the editor, the director can. His production secretary noted the exact position at the end of the last shot. They are therefore able to make sure that the teacup is held in precisely the same way and that the man himself is looking in the same direction. Small points perhaps, but points which are extremely important to an editor. When he cuts the two shots together he will quickly find any continuity errors and by then it may be too late.

I remember one particular film unit which spent a whole morning filming an interview with a retired general. In the afternoon they decided to reshoot some of the sequences they had filmed in the course of the morning. They took great care to set up the camera at a different angle so that the material exposed in the afternoon could be intercut with the morning's material without any technical problem. Unfortunately they did not notice that the general had changed his tie in the course of the lunch hour! When the material was processed and screened the difference was obvious and it was quite clear that the two batches of material could never be intercut. In this particular instance the film unit was to some extent fortunate for, after much persuasion, the general agreed to let them re-shoot the whole interview. But of course they had to meet considerable extra cost, simply because no one had paid any attention to the simplest points of continuity.

Change of Camera Angle

In the example of the general, note that the film unit took care to change the angle of the camera viewpoint. For editing this is important, and the editor's needs must be remembered when the shooting script listing camera positions is produced. Audiences are easily bored and, to maintain their interest the scenes they watch must be changed quite frequently. This presents little problem where the script calls for different places or people to be seen one after the other. But where the same subject or person is to be seen for any length of time, the angle of observation must be constantly varied. Even a simple sequence needs a variety of different shots if it is to be interesting. Long shots and close-ups and medium shots are needed as well, viewed from a variety of different angles. When the script is first written these viewpoints must be carefully selected, with the editor in mind. To cut from a view of a person from one position, to another view taken from almost exactly the same distance and position would be wrong. The action would appear to jump. But this does not mean that the whole of the scripted action must be completed in one shot. It simply means that where the scene is to be changed, a change of angle of observation is required. The script must specify what is required and the script-writer must always consider what the editor is able to do.

An editor can never cut two shots together satisfactorily if they are of the same subject taken from an almost identical position. He must go first to an alternative view and then, if necessary, back to the similar shot. As well as making this necessity clear the script must also bear in mind the main requirements of continuity. In the case of a man cleaning his car, for example, the first long shot shows the man looking from left to right. His right hand holds a polishing leather with which he cleans the bonnet of the car. He is looking down, in the direction of the leather. The second shot must match the end of the first if the editor is to be able to cut the two together smoothly. When the two exposures are made, the action of the long shot should be repeated when the camera is moved to the closer position, plus any further action required. Then the editor can select the best cutting point and join the two shots together without a jump in the action.

There is another aspect of continuity which needs attention. And here again, the editor has to rely on the script. If, after the long shot and the close up in the above example the action again turns to a long view, it must be taken from an acceptable angle. There is quite a wide choice. The man cleaning the car is still the subject of the action. He can be observed from the front or from the side, from above or from below. But direction must always be remembered. The man can look towards the camera or away from it or left to right as in the first shot. The camera must never be moved to the other side so that the man appears to have suddenly turned round and be facing right to left. The editor therefore relies on the script to give him an adequate number of shots from the right angles.

He will rely on the director to see that continuity is preserved in the course of making the exposures.

42

Overlapping Shots

When filming is in progress it always pays to overlap each shot forming part of a sequence of actions. The final action of the last shot should be re-shot from the position of the new one and any dialogue immediately preceding the cut retaken. This applies only in cases where several shots in a sequence show similar actions and involve the same characters and locations or sets. Let us consider some actual examples.

Three people are drinking in a bar. The script calls for three shots. The first is a general view of the bar in which the people are drinking. The second shows the group from a different viewpoint and there is a third in which the leader of the group is the central point. In the course of the three shots, the men are exchanging glasses of beer they have emptied for full ones. Shot one is done first. When shot two is taken, which is from a different point of view, the last actions performed by the three men in the previous shot are repeated. There are two reasons for this. The editor is able to choose his cutting point and pick the exact place to cut from shot one to shot two without fear of finding everyone in a different position. Secondly, actors, too, will be able to get into their stride better if they start with an action they are already familiar with.

Rushes

Every day, when filming has finished, the exposed materials are sent to a laboratory to be processed. They develop the material exposed in the camera and provide "rushes".[1]

This is the name given to the first rush prints made from the material exposed in the camera. The name owes its origin to the fact that first prints are usually produced very quickly. In fact these prints can normally be supplied overnight. Most directors view rushes every morning so that anything which has to be reshot can be retaken before sets are dismantled or locations cleared of equipment. The rush print will never be a guide to the results expected from your final showprint. Rushes are produced in a hurry.

The individual fluctuations in negative density and so exposure required for each shot, are not accounted for or carefully calculated. Sometimes all shots are exposed to the same printer light and a "one light" editing print is obtained. Colour material is

[1] In the U.S. the term "dailies" is widely used.

often rush printed on black and white, because monochrome prints are cheaper. When this is done, it is wise to obtain a test colour print of a few sample rolls to check quality before editing begins. The colour master can be carefully examined on a flat rewind bench in the cutting room.

Processing

Black and white negative processing techniques differ from those of colour material. It is important that the editor should understand what goes on in the processing laboratory. In his work he will often be dealing with this side of the business.

Film itself consists of a celluloid base coated with a photographic emulsion. The emulsion is made up of silver halide set in a gelatine carrier. When the silver halides are exposed to light they change, although the human eye cannot appreciate the change until the film has been processed. So the film must first of all be developed. In the course of development the silver halides which have been exposed to light are made visible by the development process. The developer is drained off, and the film is immersed in a fixing solution. This washes away those areas of silver which have not been exposed to light. The film can then be washed and dried in special air cabinets. It is then ready to be printed.

At the end of the development stage there is a negative image. This now has to be printed on a suitable positive stock. A light is shone through the negative image on to positive stock designed for the purpose. The positive is then itself developed and fixed. The developer again converts the parts of the film which have been exposed to light to black metallic silver. This time, however, the parts which are being made black are the opposite parts to those converted on the negative because this is a print from a negative. In the second stage of developing the print, those silver halides not exposed to light in the printer are washed away. The print is then washed and dried and a normal positive image with a full range of tones should result.

The laboratory has to cope with vast footages of film in this manner, and a special method of developing had to be devised. Also the rate of development has to be very carefully controlled, for it, and the temperature of the developer, are closely allied to the resultant quality. The longer a film is in the developer, the greater will be the effective sensitivity or film speed. Grain, too, becomes far more obvious and may even spoil the image. To ensure that a reel of film is properly developed for the right time, laboratories use a series of long tanks. The film is laced round rollers which are then immersed in the tanks. The film moves through the tanks at a fixed speed: about 40 ft a minute is used for some film stocks. The film then runs through a series of glass-sided warm-air cabinets, where it is dried. As it comes out of the cabinets, it is wound in a reel again, ready for the printer.

Printing Methods

There are several different kinds of motion-picture printer. In some, negative and positive are held in contact with each other. Others focus the negative image on a positive film held in a separate gate.

In the continuous type of printer, negative and positive are held in contact with one another on a large driven sprocket. Inside the sprocket is a light, which can be regulated to any of twenty-one different intensities by means of a shutter between the light source and the printer gate. The negative is held nearest the printer light and the unexposed positive runs outside it, base outwards away from the printer light.

Continuous printers normally run at speed and can print around two hundred ft of film per minute.

Another kind of contact printing machine, the step or intermittent printer, employs an intermittent mechanism to guide the two pieces of film through a gate in contact with each other. The film is moved by a claw and it advances frame by frame, though very rapidly. These machines are supposed to give a slightly steadier image and rather better definition than the continuous types. They also tend to wear out the original more quickly. And they run more slowly; around 50 ft a minute is the most an intermittent machine can cope with.

A third alternative is the optical printer. The negative here is not held in contact with the positive. Its image is projected through optics designed to throw a focused image. The size of the image projected can be varied by altering the distance between positive and negative and this kind of printer is used for producing 35 mm. blow-up prints from 16 mm. negatives and also for doing reductions. Sections of a frame can also be blown up to fill the whole frame size and various special effects can be undertaken. As the image is projected, masks can be interposed in the projected beam and such effects as views through keyholes and binoculars are sometimes produced in this manner.

When exposed materials are sent to the laboratory, requirements should be specified exactly. It is no use sending in a roll of unprocessed Ektachrome requesting a print. The laboratory want to know how the Ektachrome has been exposed and if a colour or black and white print is required. They also want to know if a full, colour corrected, graded (or "timed") print is needed or if a one light copy is satisfactory until the final edited version has been finished.

All exposed rolls of film should be identified stating clearly the film speed they have been exposed at and the name and address of the production company. Camera sheets should be included with the film and an exact specification of what is to be printed. The laboratory has to process all the camera master, but they do not have to print it all. If each shot has been clearly identified at the start of each take, they can be asked to print only takes which are worth printing. The camera sheets should contain footage indications of where these takes are to be found in the exposed rolls and of how long they are. It is normal practice to list all takes on camera sheets together with the amount of film used. A circle can then be placed round all the takes where a print is required, and the laboratory should then be asked to print only circled takes.

When the rushes have been developed and printed they are returned to the editor. Now the actual work of editing can begin.

4

EDITING EQUIPMENT AND FACILITIES

FILM editing is carried out in a room known as a cutting room. It is never elaborate. The only decoration you will find is a copy of the local fire regulations or the Factories Act if you're lucky! But the room often seems to be filled with a mass of complicated looking equipment.

The Sync. Bench

On one side of the room is a special kind of table. Hanging beneath each end of it are two linen bags. The top surface of the table has been cut away so that entry to the bags is unobstructed. Between the two bags is a square glass panel usually about 18 in. in width. It is usually opal or frosted diffusing glass and a light is located underneath it. On the extreme left-hand end of the table there is normally a large and heavy metal film horse. It consists of three or four thin but sturdy metal poles about 18 in. high and $\frac{1}{2}$ in. thick, permanently attached to a weighted metal base. A removable rod passes through the divisions of the partitions midway between the top of the poles and the weighted base. The film horse is designed to hold several reels of film side by side at the same level. Separate reels are placed in between the metal poles and the cross bar passes through the centre of each reel. Film rotates when drawn off the reels and, as there is no obstruction, leaves the horse quite freely.

At the other end of the table, to the right of the right-hand linen bag, is a geared rewind arm with an extremely long spindle. It is usually long enough to take four or five reels at a time. These are placed next to each other on the spindle separated by small springs and are held in position by a suitable clamp. Films coming from the film horses can be taken up on reels placed on this spindle without difficulty. Any slack film can be channelled into the linen bags between the two spindles. The table on which all these items are mounted, is known as a sync. bench or editing table.

Take-up arm for right-hand end of synchroniser bench showing hinged coupling on spindle and spindle rest which allows quick interchange of reels.

Synchronisers

The sync. bench takes its name from a small piece of equipment which is usually positioned on the glass panel in the middle of a sync. bench. The synchroniser is a most important piece of editing equipment and it is used at most stages of editing. It consists of a series of large sprockets permanently fixed on a rotating shaft. The film is held on the sprockets by two sprung rollers which can be raised to place film on the sprocket teeth, then lowered and locked to hold the film in position. The different sprockets on the synchroniser are rigidly mounted on a common driving shaft so they cannot be rotated independently. Two pieces of film placed in level synchronisation,[1] that is to say, with certain frames opposite one another and locked on to the teeth of the sprockets, will remain synchronised whichever way the sprockets are revolved. When the synchroniser is placed on the illuminated glass panel in the middle of the sync. bench, light can shine through the film placed in the synchroniser thus making it possible to see the image on the film. A footage counter is also a standard part of every synchroniser. This counts the footage of film passing through the synchroniser, will work in either direction and can be reset to zero. Synchronisers are made for 16 mm. and for 35 mm. film. The number of sprockets on a synchroniser varies between models. Four-sprocket model (the four way) and a six-way are the most common, but there are also two-way versions. Models that can handle 16 mm. and 35 mm. together are also in wide use. The 16 mm. sprockets are mounted alongside 35 mm.

[1] *U.S. term "editorial sync." see page 145.*

sprockets, and are appropriately geared down so that 16 mm. film placed in level synchronisation with 35 mm. will remain "in synch." when the two pieces of film are wound through the synchroniser together. The difference in the location of the 35 mm. and 16 mm. sprocket teeth, and the subsequent slight difference in the diameter of the sprocket, compensate for the different film dimensions. Synchronisers are never powered. To move film on the sprockets you use a small wheel, mounted on the end of the driving shaft. Alternatively, film placed on the synchroniser can be taken up on a spool at the right hand side of the sync. bench. When tension on the film is increased, it will pass through the synchroniser quite freely.

The synchroniser is used for many editing operations. As its purpose is to make it possible to keep a number of different pieces of film in synchronisation with each other, it can be used for preserving synchronisation between picture and separate magnetic soundtracks. It is also useful for matching the edited cutting copy of your final edited version to the master material. Some modern synchronisers have a small viewing screen above the front sprocket so that the editor can see a projected picture from film placed on the front sprocket.

Many models have small magnetic soundheads attached to the second, third and fourth sprockets of a four-way model. These can be connected to a small amplifier and speaker unit. Sound recorded on the various soundtracks used in the synchroniser can be heard. These soundheads are needed from the outset when editing sync. takes and rushes as we shall see later on.

To summarise then: the synchroniser is essential for editing. It can be used for the synchronisation of picture to picture, or picture to soundtrack. Its purpose is to ensure that film placed in level synchronisation on a synchroniser's sprockets, remains in sync. until it is removed. The basic equipment consists of a series of large sprockets. These sprockets are locked on a common driving shaft which can be propelled by hand, or driven by taking up slack film on spools placed on the right of the synchroniser, and gradually increasing the tension of the film until the wheels of the synchroniser begin to move. A footage, and sometimes a frame counter, is also fitted to the basic equipment. A picture-viewing screen is sometimes attached to the front sprocket. The remaining tracks are often equipped with either a fixed or a detachable soundhead for replaying sound when sprocketed magnetic soundtracks are wound through the synchroniser. Such soundheads are connected with a separate small amplifier unit which has its own volume control.

Editing Machines

The term "editing machine"[1] is much abused. To an amateur film maker it means anything from a second-rate tape splicer, itself almost held together with tape, to some kind of animated viewer. To the professional it has far more significance, for the professional editor will rely on a machine to help him in his work.

The purpose of an editing machine is, unlike so many machines in industry today, to help a highly skilled technician, the film editor, to do a job where he always remains in control.

There are two main kinds of editing machine. Those on which you can see only a projected picture, and those which, in addition to projecting the image of the film also provide for the reproduction of soundtracks. The various types of equipment available are suited to different uses.

Animated Viewers

The small factory film unit may have to make do with a small animated viewer. It probably consists of a few rollers and a small viewing screen, usually three or four inches across, on which the picture is projected by rotating via a prism. This kind of viewer is often fitted on a small baseboard, on which two rewind arms are mounted. To move film through the gate of the viewer you increase the tension on the film which is fed from one rewind arm, via the viewer, to the other. The speed at which the film can be viewed therefore depends entirely on the speed at which the rewind arms are operated. As the arms are not power operated, but are controlled by hand, it is almost impossible to gauge the duration of any shot accurately. These machines are certainly not suitable for any advanced kind of editing. The animated viewer may, however, be useful in the first stages of editing. You can assemble shots in the right order, for editing to length later on. Then a power-driven machine can be brought in to see exactly how long each shot lasts at the speed at which the finished film will be projected. If you have to view several thousand feet of film, looking for one suitable shot, the viewer may be quite convenient. You can speed through what you don't want to see, and slow down when you reach the vicinity of the wanted shot. For these purposes the very controllable hand-operated viewer has its merits. But where the best possible job of

[1] *See glossary note page 144.*

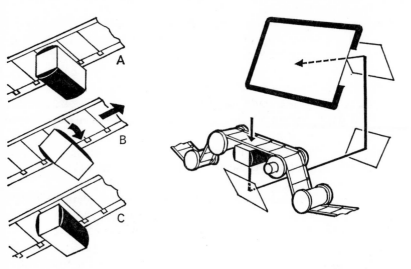

The viewer, where a picture is back projected on a small screen via a rotating prism.

editing is to be done on any film, this elementary equipment must be augmented by something rather more versatile.

Some models of animated viewer are much more expensive than others and I have found that for my purposes one of the cheaper ones gives excellent performance. The viewer is made of metal and is reasonably sturdy. It folds up conveniently if you want to move it and gives a good bright picture on a ground-glass screen. The film passes under two guide rollers the second of which is directly above a sprocket. This sprocket turns a rotating prism immediately under the film gate. A light shines through the film to the prism and the picture is then thrown on to a ground-glass screen. The small lamp-

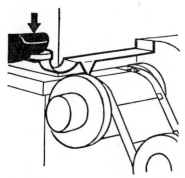

Some animated viewers incorporate a notching device for marking individual frames.

51

house can be raised and lowered by hand to give direct access to the film in the picture gate. When the lamphouse is raised the lamp itself cuts out and, after marking the film in the appropriate place, the lamphouse is simply lowered again and the lamp switches itself on. Before choosing a machine like this, look at the quality of the picture. Check that it is clear and sharp and bright enough to look at all day without getting tired. Be sure you do not have to peer through the mirk to see any kind of picture. The film must be easy to mark, without having to burn your fingers on the lamp or turn the machine on its side. Admittedly, these are small points but they are important ones when working on a machine for any length of time.

With the animated viewer which is always hand operated, a firm baseboard is needed and two suitable rewind arms. It is worth spending a little extra money to get two sturdy rewind arms. Despite the higher initial expense in this case it will probably work out cheaper in the long run. When choosing rewind arms look for the pitfalls. How do the reels fit on to them? Do they clip on, slide on, or stay on by faith and hope? Some rewind arms contain a small spring set into the centre of the spindle over which the spool slots. This system is quite good if the spring is a strong one that will stand up to the wear and tear of hundreds of reels being clipped on to it and pulled off again. An alterative method is to buy an arm where the spindle has been hinged in the end section. You slide your reel on the spindle and then turn the end upwards as a buffer to stop the reel falling off again. This is an excellent system, again provided that the spindle is a sturdy one. Look for something strong. And make sure the gears are well proportioned so you don't have to turn the handle at a feverish pace to take up a reel of film. Let the gearing do the hard work for you.

Projectors in Editing

A shot must be seen projected at the correct speed in the later stages of editing. This may perhaps suggest that a projector would be a good companion for the animated viewer as basic film cutting equipment. Unfortunately, projectors are not suitable for editing. They are designed for continuous projection and not for constant stopping and starting and moving in all directions. Few projectors could stand the wear and tear imposed by advanced editing procedures. No projector is capable of doing the operations for which editing equipment is needed. An editing machine must be sturdily built. The picture gate must also be readily accessible because a cutting point has to be marked on the film with a wax pencil before a cut is made. This becomes a major operation on most projectors where gates normally open only 45 degrees. In editing, one frame of inaccuracy can be very significant. In a quick action sequence one frame can be the difference between a good cut and a bad one. On one shot of a man running at speed, his right foot may be forward on one frame of film and level with his left foot in the next. To find the exact cutting point you need a machine accurate to one frame. It must be stopped without difficulty with the right frame showing at the right time in the most accessible place. A projector does not allow the editor to control the movement of the film accurately enough. Stopping with a precise frame on the screen is a complicated business and, with many projectors, it is impossible. Even if you do manage to get the right frame in the picture gate, there is a likelihood of it being turned to a blister by a powerful projection lamp.

Although projectors are not designed for editing work, at some stages of the operation they are undoubtedly useful. All rushes and newly photographed material should be projected first before being run on an editing machine. The projector will give a fair idea of the quality of the material. Editing machines are usually designed for editing and not specifically to enable someone to view and judge quality. A projector may also be employed on occasions in the later stages of editing. I personally always like to see the rough cut on a projector and a large size screen. I use a Siemens projector which projects the mute cutting copy on one side and the edited magnetic track on the other. This is very satisfactory for the purpose. It helps me to gauge the pace of the film. I can see at a glance when the film is projected without stopping, where one shot is longer or shorter than it should be. I find it is worth running the cutting copy on a projector at the end of each stage of making an edited version. But I rely on an editing machine for the actual editing operation.

Two-Speed Machine

The editing machine must first of all show a picture of reasonable quality. The picture must be clear, reasonably steady, and large enough for you to be able to appreciate details like footsteps and lip movements, all of which can be of vital importance when sound editing is in progress. The machine should be able to show film at normal speed and at double speed. One which can run at normal sound speed of 24 frames per second is essential but it is certainly a great advantage if the same machine will also run at double speed.

53

You may find your editing print interesting the first few hundred times you see it. But when you have to run through the whole thing from the beginning, to find a point some way in from the start of the reel, you will soon grow tired of waiting for the scene you are concerned with to appear. A machine which can speed through material you are not immediately concerned with will be welcome, and will probably save time and money in the course of production.

Sound Facilities

Having chosen for preference a machine which runs pictures at normal and double speed, with acceptable standards of picture illumination and steadiness, next you have to decide on the kind of sound you wish to edit.

Most power-operated editing machines are built to accommodate a reel of picture and one or more separate magnetic soundtracks. If you are working with a 16 mm. picture you may wish to use only 16 mm. soundtracks, but this is by no means essential. Most makers of 16 mm. editing machines also produce a 16/35 model. This is not as complex as it sounds. The term 16/35 simply means that with a 16 mm. picture it is possible to run either a 35 mm. soundtrack or a 16 mm. one. Some models will take one, and some the other. The choice does not lie entirely with you. The sound dubbing theatre, where you will eventually mix your soundtracks together, will ultimately determine the kind of tracks you use. Ask them how many replay soundheads they have for each gauge of soundtrack, and this information will have a considerable bearing on the type of track you use for editing.

Most dubbing theatres can accommodate a 16 mm. picture, and nowadays a considerable number can also provide facilities for reproducing and re-recording a number of tracks of 16 mm. sound. Some, however, can still only cope with 35 mm. tracks, although they are perfectly happy to project a 16 mm. picture. Check before you edit anything, and you will then be able to make sure you use the most suitable stock and equipment.

There are many kinds of power-operated editing machines for simultaneous editing of sound and picture. Let us consider their main characteristics.

Editing machines can be very expensive. Several models cost more than a sound camera unit and unlike many makes of animated viewer most machines are built to do a job rather than to meet a price. At the lower end of the price range there are machines capable

54

of running 16 mm. picture with 16 mm. sound at both normal and double speeds. The Acmade Miniola is a good example of this type of equipment. It is an upright model, which simply means that the picture feed and take-up plates are placed immediately above those used for magnetic film and the picture runs from left to right immediately above the magnetic track. Magnetic and optical soundtracks can be reproduced on this machine and, for the price, quality of sound reproduction is quite reasonable. The picture is shown on a small eye-level screen and the brilliance of the image can be controlled. Sound can be moved without moving the picture by using a simple sprocket disengagement device. If you want to move the action and not the sound, this too can be done by using a similar sprocket disengagement device on the driving sprocket of the picture.

For a small film unit this machine is quite a good investment.

Another popular machine, again produced by the Acmade Company, is the Acmade editing table. Here picture and sound run horizontally parallel to each other, across what is virtually a table. Film is passed from left hand feed spools or plates, through a driving sprocket, over a soundhead or through a picture gate, via another sprocket out to take-up spools or plates. The picture is projected through a rotating prism located immediately above the picture gate. To thread up the film, you simply lift the prism unit to one side, and thread the film from one of the driving sprockets to the other. The whole operation could not be simpler. Again it is possible to project either optical or magnetic sound. A number of 35 mm. and 16 mm. models are produced. Here again it is quite easy to obtain a model with 16 mm. picture and 16 or 35 mm. sound. The picture quality of these editing tables is quite good and the quality of sound reproduction suitable for use with speech and effects recordings. It is an exceedingly simple machine to use and much editing work can be undertaken using this equipment.

A larger and more expensive machine is the Steenbeck editing table. Again, this is an editing table, though there the resemblance between the Steenbeck and the Acmade comes to an end. At first sight the top of the Steenbeck table appears very complex, for the film path is not particularly simple. The quality of sound and picture reproduction however is superb. Steenbecks are rather more expensive than some editing machines; in fact, the Miniola is less than half the price of the Steenbeck, and naturally you would expect greater versatility from the more expensive machine. The picture is back projected on a large eye-level screen. Sound runs nearest the editor and picture runs, almost parallel, at the back of the machine. The threading has been simplified in recent years and the machine can now be threaded quickly and with ease. The magnetic track can be disengaged from the machine's driving mechanism without unthreading the film and it is thus possible to alter the relative positions of sound and picture at will. Sound can be advanced or retarded and synchronisation can then be restored by relocking the two film paths to the drive mechanism. The machine uses a quartz iodine lamp, which gives a good quality picture, and recent models have sliding volume and tone controls. There are separate control buttons for forward and reverse running and also for double speed. These controls can be operated by hand or by using foot pedals. A slow-motion inching foot pedal control is also fitted. Film is held horizontally on plates which will accept 2,000 feet of film mounted either on spools or on plastic cores. Footage counters and a variety of useful accessories are supplied as extras.

Which is the best equipment to use?

Every editor has his favourite kind of equipment. If it is possible, he should use the machine he personally finds best for the kind of work he does.

Before you can edit a film you will need to mark the point at which you want to make your cut on the film itself. An ordinary pen or pencil will not, of course, write on film, so a wax pencil, such as a Chinagraph, is used. A supply of these is a basic part of cutting-room equipment. When you have marked your cutting point you will also need scissors to cut the film. Again these are basic items of cutting-room equipment. Brass scissors are most suitable because they are anti-magnetic and will not impair the quality of magnetic soundtracks. Other kinds of scissors are satisfactory provided precautions are taken to make the scissors anti-magnetic before they are used to cut magnetic soundtracks. When the film has been marked up and cut it must be spliced in the manner chosen. To do this a film splicer will be needed.

Film Splices

There are two main methods of joining film: with a liquid solution called film cement, or with transparent tape. Both are used by professional editors in the course of editing a production. Some editors despise tape splices, but most of them use a tape splicer during the early stages of the editing process. When splicing with tape, you do not have to allow for the loss of a number of frames as is the case with the conventional type of film splicer where an overlap type of splice is produced.

With the cement splicer, film is cut and the emulsion is scraped off a small part of the edge of one frame on one side of the splice. Cement is applied to the clear film and the piece of film to be spliced to it is brought in contact with the cement-coated clear film before it has a chance to dry and harden. The second piece of film is not scraped clear of emulsion. If it were to be scraped clear, the two pieces would allow light from the projector lamp to pass straight through the film. At that point a white flash would appear on the screen. The second piece of film is, however, cut to a slightly different length to allow a small part of the edge of the last frame to overlap the part of the other piece of film from which the emulsion has been scraped. The two pieces of film are therefore virtually welded together with film cement.

In a tape splice the system is entirely different. When splicing with tape no overlap is needed. The two pieces of film are cut and laid end to end so that they touch each other but do not overlap. One piece of transparent adhesive tape is then placed across both ends of film and the sprocket holes are punched clear of the tape. You need neither cement nor patience, for the splice is completed in a second.

Both systems have advantages and disadvantages. As frames are lost when splicing with cement, it is rather difficult to change any cut. But if you have spliced with tape you will not have any problem.

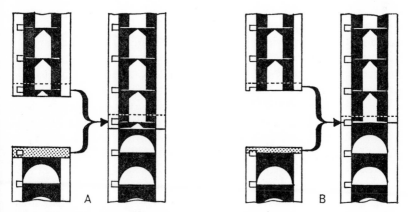

When splicing 16 mm. film with a cement splice a small overlap (B) is preferable when splicing most materials. The larger overlap (A) will give added strength to a splice, but will also appear more obvious when the film is projected.

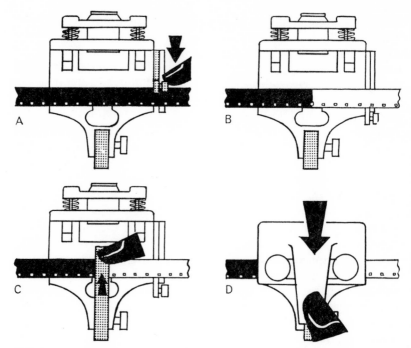

Stages in the operation of a tape splicer. (A) Place one piece of film across splicer with point at which you wish to cut on right-hand edge and bring knife down to cut it. (B) Move pieces of film you wish to splice to the centre of splicer. (C) Cover both pieces with tape. (D) Bring down top of splicer to cut tape and clear sprocket holds.

Simply peel off the tape and splice where you wish. It is for precisely this reason that I always use tape splices when I am editing a cutting copy and cement splices when doing anything else.

Cement splices are imperative for master materials. They are recommended for projection prints because tape splices are rather thicker than cement ones and some projectors take a disliking to this sudden increase in the film thickness. Cement splices can be almost invisible when projected. Tape splices can always be noticed because the tape must cover two or more frames, and, although it is transparent, as time goes by it discolours. For editing magnetic soundtracks I find tape splices unbeatable as you can splice straight across the track or diagonally.

Whichever method of splicing you use always make sure you are using good materials. Choose tape made for the job. Remember as the tape has to pass through delicate editing equipment, it must be reasonably strong and thin. When you have completed your tape splice, check that the edges of the film have been properly trimmed and pieces of loose tape are not clogging the sprocket holes. Always use tape on the cellulose (shiny) side of the film or soundtrack and never put tape on the emulsion. With cement, be certain that the cement you are using is fresh. It doesn't keep for ever. In a large studio cement is changed every morning. Keep the splicer free of stray pieces of film and always cork up the cement bottle immediately after making a splice. This will prevent the air shortening the life of the cement left in the bottle.

Cement Splicers

There are a number of different kinds of cement splicer. A well-equipped cutting-room will probably have a large foot-operated splicer which can be used for 35 mm. and 16 mm. film. These splicers undoubtedly make the finest possible kind of cement splice and, with just a little practice, are easy to use at speed. They are, however, weighty and cannot be described as portable. A more common kind of splicer incorporates an automatic scraper. You simply place the pieces of film you want to join on two sets of sprockets, end to end. One operation cuts the film to length, another scrapes the emulsion from one side of one of the ends of film and the two pieces are then brought in contact with each other. The whole operation is accomplished in a matter of seconds. The cement is put on the film by a small rotating wheel which is immersed in a well of cement. You do not need to scrape the film or apply cement with a brush: the machine takes care of the whole operation. You simply operate two handles which in turn control the various actions.

The smaller film unit may have to make do with a much smaller splicer. This is not necessarily a disadvantage. Although making a splice with this kind of equipment may take a few seconds longer than with a foot splicer or the machine just described, the resulting splice can be just as good and quite as durable. Always try to use a 16 mm. splicer designed to make a small splice—not one which will effectively take up one or more frames of picture. If possible, use a splicer where the splicing block is heated for this will speed up the whole operation and assist in bonding together the two pieces of film. Scrape the film with care. Some people like to scrape the back of the opposite piece of film to ensure that the splice really does hold and this practice is worth while, although care must be taken not to scrape too deeply. The purpose of scraping the opposite side of a splice is simply to lose any wax coating or other foreign matter which

59

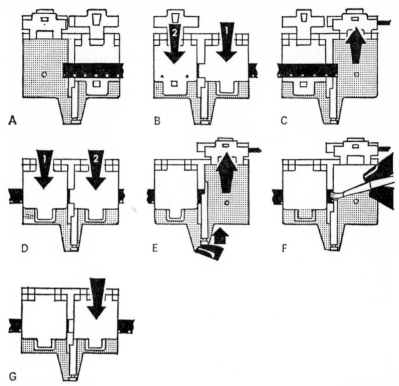

Stages in the operation of a cement splicer. (A) Place one piece of film on right-hand side of splicer. (B) Lower top of right-hand side and bring left-hand side down to cut the film opposite. (C) Raise right-hand side again and insert film on left side. (D) Bring right-hand side down again to cut film on left. (E) Raise right-hand side and scrape piece of left side still visible. (F) Apply cement to left side portion. (G) Bring right side down in contact with wet cement. Wait 10 secs., release both sides and inspect.

might interfere with the splice. Before you attempt to stick anything, place the film in the splicer and cut it to length, then wipe off any wax pencil marks on the area to be spliced for they will make the splice fall apart.

Ancillary Equipment

The rest of the cutting-room equipment is comparatively insignificant. Some film bins[1] (film barrels) are needed. These are large metal or fibre bins lined with linen bags. Above these bins are editing racks, clips or pegs from which individual shots can be suspended. At the start of editing a film you will first of all need to

[1] *See glossary note page 145.*

60

break the rushes down to individual shots. Shots can then be suspended in these bins, suitably numbered with grease pencil marks on the film and on top of the bins. When a cut has been made, the part of the shot not used, known as the trim or out-take, is returned to these bins. Hence the name, trim bins. In the cutting-room you will find a waste bin which is used for throwing away film not required.

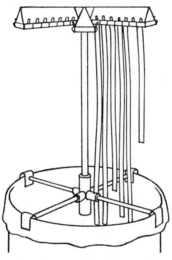

The trim bin shots are sorted into order and held by numbered clips on the cross bars
Other ends hang inside the linen bag which prevents damage.

A flat rewind table is also needed. This consists simply of two large plates for holding film, set on either side of an illuminated glass inspection panel. It is called a flat rewind because the plates on which film is placed are horizontal and not vertical. Film is laid flat on plates. This kind of rewind is especially useful for rewinding negative, where particular care must be taken. A series of racks for cans of film and basic materials completes the cutting-room equipment. White spacing, clear film and black framed opaque film are all basic materials you need.

Cutting-room Layout

The arrangement of equipment in a cutting-room is an important factor for efficient working conditions. The main consideration is of course to make everything accessible and convenient. You should not have to trail a piece of film right across the cutting-room from your editing machine to the splicer every time you want to make a splice. Also, you should not have to look under everything or stand on a chair each time you want to find a can of film. Make sure that, whenever possible, the light from any window in the cutting-room shines sideways across the editing machine and does not come from in front of it or from behind. If it is from behind the bright light may obscure the picture completely and if it faces the editor he will find it difficult to concentrate. Here are two suggested arrangements.

Put your sync. bench by the window of the cutting-room and alongside it place the trim bin. On the right-hand side at right angles to the sync. bench you can put the editing machine, and on the right of that you will have space for the splicer. Straightaway you

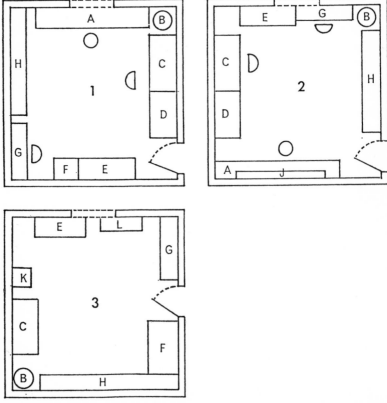

Cutting-room layouts. (A) Sync. bench (in window). (B) Trim bin. (C) Editing machine. (D) Splicer. (E) Viewer. (F) Table. (G) Flat rewind. (H) Racks. (J) Trim bin attached to wall. (K) Hand splicer. (L) Foot-operated splicer.

have established a kind of production line. The editing machine and the splicer are alongside one another so you won't have to drag film all over the floor every time you want to make a splice. This, of course, applies to a large cement splicer and not the smaller cement splicer or tape splicer, which can itself be placed on top of the editing machine. Against the wall opposite the editing machine you will have room for a number of film racks, and the flat rewind. You can position the animated viewer on a table next to the flat rewind. Chairs in front of the table and the editing machine, together with a high stool in front of the sync. bench should not take up too much space and will make it possible to work in comfort.

An alternative way of setting out a cutting-room is to place the viewer and a flat rewind bench in the window and position the sync. bench along the opposite wall. A trim bin can then be built along the wall behind the sync. bench, which should be left about 1 ft from the actual wall. You can put the splicer at one end of the sync. bench and alongside occupying another wall, the editing machine. This leaves one wall free for film racks and the waste bin. Everything is thus accessible and the three main pieces of equipment—editing machine, sync. bench and splicer—are within easy reach of each other. Careful planning and arrangement of equipment will save time and make editing much easier.

Cutting-room Hire

Some small film units, particularly those forming part of an industrial concern, may find they are unable to meet the considerable cost of equipping a cutting-room. They may perhaps be able to afford an animated viewer and a splicer but they cannot justify the considerably extra cost of advanced editing equipment. They have to decide if they are going to settle for a simple edited film, completed on inadequate equipment, or if they wish to hire a ready-equipped cutting-room. Most large film companies have such cutting-rooms for hire. You simply have to make enquiries.

Do not just look for a cutting-room which is available for hire, but make sure that it is the right kind of cutting-room for your particular film. Not all cutting-rooms can cope with both 16 mm. and 35 mm. film. Check first and see that the equipment is the right gauge. Do they have a range of good equipment and does it work, or is it in a poor condition? Does the company hiring out the cutting-room agree to undertake all necessary maintenance and repairs to equipment and, if so, are you going to be charged with the cost?

These are the first points to check if you ever hire a cutting-room. It is also worth looking into the question of the other facilities you require. You will need a dubbing theatre, a projection theatre and possibly a titling studio. How can these best be hired?

A cutting-room is normally hired on a weekly basis. A set sum is charged per week for the use of the cutting-room and all equipment. You will not get any staff for that sum and will have to do your own editing and obtain your own assistant. You will also have to provide any raw materials you use such as spacing, leader and opaque film.

Dubbing-Theatre Hire

When you hire a dubbing theatre, the situation is quite different. First of all you need the dubbing theatre for a very much shorter time, possibly only a matter of hours. The exact amount of time depends on the number of soundtracks you have and how complicated they are for the sound mixer who will blend them together. For a simple thirty-minute film with one track of music and one track of commentary an hour and a half is ample. If you have five tracks of sound effects and two of music as well as three of dialogue the same length film could take at least a day to complete. If you are in doubt about the amount of time needed, ask the dubbing-theatre sound mixer: the man who will actually do the job. Tell him what you want him to work with and ask his advice. This is far better than guessing yourself and ending up with a half-finished dubbed sequence at the end of your booked time in the theatre.

When you hire a dubbing theatre you hire it complete with staff. You have a sound mixer and one or more sound recordists. They lace your edited soundtracks on reproducing machines and also load a reel of blank stock on a recording machine. A projectionist completes the dubbing-theatre crew. He threads up the cutting copy picture and watches it pass through the projector to make sure it doesn't fall apart! Dubbing theatres can be hired by the hour and the charge made includes the services of all the staff and the equipment.

One important point to check when you book a dubbing theatre is the number of tracks the theatre can cope with at any one time. How many tracks can they run with your edited picture? Can they run two or ten? If they can only run two and you have five tracks, the film will have to be run through four times. On the first run two tracks are mixed together; on the second, one more can be added and so on. It takes much longer than it would in a dubbing theatre which can cope with ten tracks. There they can, if they wish, mix all the tracks at once, though the mixer may not choose to do so. It's quite normal practice to mix together sound effects first then go through again and add music and finally add dialogue. This may sound a waste of time, but it isn't. If the mixer mixes his sound effects together first of all he will know when he starts to add the music exactly how loud it must be at any point. He will know if a scene is going to include many sound effects or if there is to be only music. He can gauge his sound recording level and fades accordingly. After mixing the music and effects together he can add the dialogue. He will then have only the dialogue tracks and one combined music and effects track to cope with, and the operation will be considerably easier. This system of mixing the tracks piece by piece is known as pre-mixing.

When you book a dubbing theatre you should also ascertain which gauge of soundtrack they are accustomed to handle. Not all dubbing theatres can cope with 16 mm. soundtracks. Some can run a 16 mm. picture but only 35 mm. soundtracks, and others will not handle 16 mm. at all. You should check to see how many 16 mm. soundtracks the theatre can cope with and book a theatre which is most suited to your own particular needs. When you have found the right theatre you will probably wish to use it regularly. A mixer gets used to working with an editor and it helps if each understands the other's problems and objectives.

Titling Studios

You may also require a titling studio. Here again, choose with caution. It's a good idea, first of all, to see examples of the work the studio has produced. Don't just ask to be shown examples of their work—make sure they show you a job similar in nature to the one they might undertake for you. There is no point in looking at wonderful 70 mm. title sequences if you want the same studio to make up some diagrams for a 16 mm. documentary. They may be the world's best 70 mm. title makers, but they may have no interest whatever in 16 mm. Make sure they are capable of doing the job you want them to do and see that they have suitable equipment.

You will not need to hire a titling studio. The normal procedure is to pay for each title or diagram or for a title sequence. The studio will give you a quotation for each title card. The quotation will include the work of an artist to produce the lettering on the card and any arty background you may require. It will also include the cameraman's time shooting the card and the film stock on which he shoots it. The cost of processing the material may or may not be included and you should always ask if the price includes supplying a processed original and an editing print.

5

MECHANICS OF EDITING VISUALS

WE have seen in Chapter 1 how there are two methods of recording film sound when simultaneous shooting is taking place. Sound can be recorded either on a magnetic stripe alongside the actual piece of film in the camera, or on a separate piece of magnetic film or $\frac{1}{4}''$ tape, locked to the camera by sync. pulse for sync. takes, or working independently for wild recordings. We have also seen how, when a synchronised take is photographed, the top and bottom of a clapper board are banged together before the action of a scene is commenced.

When the film enters the cutting-rooms it comes in two separate cans. One is the sound, the other is the picture, or action, as it is usually known in cutting-rooms. Before editing can begin the two pieces of film must be resynchronised so that the results of the day's shooting can be viewed. The two pieces of film, one of sound and one of picture, are both known as rushes.

Synchronising Rushes

First of all you should prepare all the items of equipment you will need. You require a synchroniser equipped with a track reader to reproduce the soundtrack to be synchronised. You also need a film horse, and two spools on which to take up the synchronised rushes, together with a splicer to rejoin them ready for projection. Begin by taking the reel of picture supplied by the laboratories and putting it in the first track of the film horse. Put the reel of magnetic sound next to it. Make sure that it leaves the horse with the emulsion side (the dull one) uppermost and the sprocket holes on the same side as the teeth on the synchroniser. The magnetic material must leave the horse emulsion outwards. The emulsion side must be the right way up for a magnetic reproducing head attached to the top of the synchroniser to pick up the sound recorded on the track. Some modern synchronisers have magnetic heads built into them, set in the middle of the sprockets. If your synchroniser is one of these more modern models, magnetic tracks should leave the film horse cell (shiny side) out. In any case, whichever model you use, make sure that the track leaves the horse in such a way that the emulsion side of the track will come in contact with the magnetic reproduction head on the synchroniser.

Place the magnetic film on the teeth of the second track of the synchroniser and lock it in position. Now, adjust the volume of the track reader and move the magnetic film across the head. You should soon hear evidence of a recording. Now is the time to refer to the sound recordists information sheets and to the camera sheets provided by the cameraman and the continuity secretary. See what this reel should contain and then you will know what to look for. After winding through a few feet you should hear a voice identifying the first take you want. It will simply state the scene or take number, and will be followed by a bang on the track. This bang is, of course, the noise of the two parts of the clapper board coming in contact with each other. Wind the track very slowly and carefully over the magnetic head in the synchroniser and mark with a cross the exact point

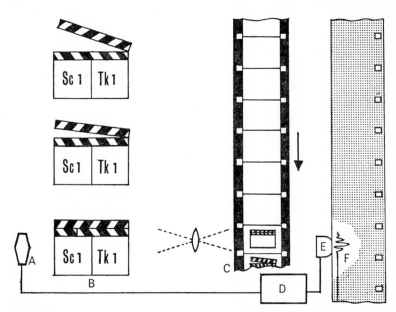

Synchronising sound and picture. The clapper board fully closed at B recorded on film at C, sends signal via microphone A and amplifier D to head E registering signal on magnetic film F.

where the bang starts, filling one frame and no more. Alongside your mark, write the scene and take number with a wax pencil. Now look at the picture.

Somewhere you will find a series of frames picturing the clapper board with the same scene and take number as you have just heard on the track. Look at it carefully and find the exact point in the action where the two sections of the clapper board meet. Mark the frame with a cross and the scene number and take. Open the synchroniser again and put your two marks opposite each other. Sound and picture are now synchronised. To be more precise they are in "level synchronisation" or level sync., as everyone says in a studio. Now you can splice some white spacing film on the sound and picture, taking care to splice on the right-hand side of the synchroniser. When they have been attached, wind back and put a large start mark on both pieces of film at the same point. A start mark takes the form of a large cross on the picture and three straight lines or a large cross on the soundtrack. It should occupy only one frame. Mark at the head of the roll the title of the film and the fact that this is reel one, then place the ends of the spacing in take-up spools and wind on. As the wax pencil marks on the clapper board pass through the synchroniser, check again to make sure they are still level, then wind on. You can carry on winding until the end of the take. Then either sound will go dead or you will run out of picture. You will lose synchronisation at that point as filming was discontinued. Mark a level cutting point on both sound and picture and remove the picture from the synchroniser. Wind on the sound by hand until you hear the sound identification of the next scene and take number. Find the appropriate scene on the action and again mark up the clap on the soundtrack and the corresponding point in the action. Replace the action in the synchroniser, making sure that the two wax pencil marks identifying the start of this second scene and take are level. Now you can wind back until you come to the wax pencil cutting point you have already marked on the magnetic track. Put a mark on the action of the new shot at this point. Now you can join the first shot to the second. If you join on the two points you have marked, you will be sure to have both scenes in synchronisation. You can then carry on in this manner to the end of the reel.

There are several points to remember when synchronising rushes. First of all, never take off the identification. You should not attempt to make an artistic job of it. Synchronising rushes is like sandpapering woodwork before painting—a necessary but dull part of the operation. Always check your camera and sound information sheets

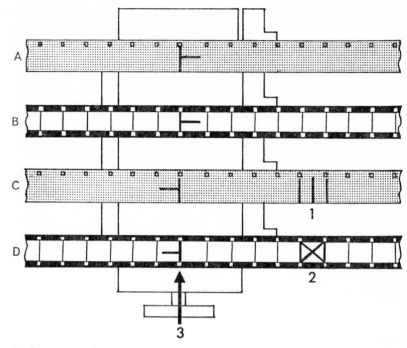

Synchronising rushes: cut from first to second sync. shot. (C) Outgoing magnetic sound. (D) Outgoing picture. (A) Incoming magnetic. (B) Incoming picture. (I and 2) Sync. marks. (3) Synchroniser hand-turning wheel.

carefully. Sometimes you will find the clapper board is on the end of a take and you have to synchronise the scene from the end and work backwards. A few minutes spent looking at the information sheets will save hours of searching for clapper boards at points where they have never been photographed.

Do not expect to find every scene that has been shot. By no means all photographed scenes are printed by the laboratory. If a scene is no good the cameraman will mark on his sheets a large N.G. At the end of the day's filming, the cameraman will go through his sheets and mark the takes which the laboratory is to print. Only these takes will reach you in positive form, although everything filmed will be on the processed master material. The same situation applies with sound. If the film has been photographed in a studio, the chances are that the sound will have been recorded straight on magnetic film. If, however, much of the work has been done on location, sound will probably have been recorded on magnetic tape and transferred to magnetic film after filming has been completed.

Here again, not all takes will have been transferred. You can save yourself the search for scenes and takes which do not exist by looking at the information sheet when you start to synchronise the rushes.

When sound and picture match exactly, the reels of film are taken to a preview theatre. In a large studio every morning the director, editor and other leading technicians and members of the cast sit and view the rushes. The director decides which takes he wishes to use and which scenes he wants to shoot again. At the end of the viewing the editor will possibly be given a rough outline of the takes he would like the editor to use. The editor can then return to the cutting-room and start making his first rough assembly.

Very few films consist only of synchronised dialogue sequences. Usually most parts of a documentary film are non-sync. and, very often in the case of an industrial or television film, the entire production is shot without sound. The addition of sound is left to the editor, as is the assembly of the action. How do you start making your first rough assembly?

Breaking Down Rushes

When the rushes have been viewed you can return to the cutting-room and start breaking down the rushes. Wind through and separate each scene and possibly each take. On the start of the scene write, with a wax pencil, the scene and take number, and then hang the length of film in the trim bin. If it is a very long piece it may be coiled up and held together with an elastic band. All scenes must be checked against the script, or if there is no script, listed on a detailed shot list. Mark the type of shot, whether long shot or close up, the subject and the action and then hang it up. Mark the number on the film itself and on the trim bin above the clip on which it hangs. As you break down each scene, make sure that the laboratory has printed through the key numbers on the edge of the film. These numbers are vital when you come to match the edited cutting print to your master material. If you find they are missing before you start to cut, send the reel of print back with the appropriate reel of negative to the laboratory. They will then number the two in ink and return them to you as soon as possible. Anyone who has had the misfortune to edit a film which has not been edge numbered, and then been faced with the need for further prints, will agree that this simple check of the rushes before cutting begins is well worth while.

Checking the Negative

Let us assume first of all that the film you are editing has been photographed without any synchronised sound. You are presented with several cans of mute print and the corresponding amount of negative. Before you do anything else, check the negative to make sure that it is all there. It may be several weeks before you actually need to use the negative again. By that time your print will be in an entirely different form and you will be unable to remember if there were originally ten or twenty rolls. Looking for material mislaid several weeks before is always a complicated and unsatisfying task. When you are satisfied that the right number of reels of negative and print have been delivered, it is quite a good idea to wind through the negative on a flat rewinder. This should be done with immense care. Always wear white linen gloves when you are working with negative, for any mark you put on the negative will remain there and blemish all prints made from the material thereafter. Negative must never be projected. It can be wound from one reel to another on the flat rewind. Hold your left hand on the extreme edges of the film and you will feel the point where the reels of negative removed from the camera have been spliced together by the processing laboratory. The laboratory when processing the exposed materials, develop each reel and then splice the various short reels together to make a more acceptable length with which to load the printing machines. Normally a laboratory will join up a number of 100 ft rolls, but the same laboratory may well leave 400 ft rolls in single rolls. They will not in any sense cut the rolls. Blank spacing and fogged scenes will all be left on. When they have an acceptable length roll they will load the film on the printer and produce your cutting print.

Noting Key Numbers

When you have placed the negative on the flat rewinder, equip yourself with a pen or pencil and a few sheets of paper. Look at the first shot on the head of the roll and find the first clear key number marked on the edge of the frame. Wind on one foot and check the next number. It should be one number higher than the number you have just noticed at the head of the roll. When you are sure that you have the right number, make a note of it on the piece of paper. You can now wind on until you feel a splice. At this point two reels of negative will have been joined together. As the two reels were originally separate, they will have a different set of key numbers. They may perhaps have been a different kind of raw stock. In this case the prefix letters as well as the number itself will have altered. First of all check the outgoing number of the roll of negative when you have just reached the end. Note the last three or four figures on your sheet of paper. Now you can note the first and last numbers of the next roll and proceed in this manner to the end of the reel. When you have noted all the numbers on the roll, rewind the negative and carefully replace it in its can. Attach the piece of paper on which you have written the numbers to the top of the can.

The purpose of this exercise is now quite apparent. Now, you can see at a glance which rolls of negative are to be found in that can. If a shot on the cutting copy is badly damaged and a reprint is needed, you will not have to wind through every roll checking each shot. You simply look at the cans until you find a roll with the right kind of number. This ease of recognition will prove immensely helpful when you come to order special effects, like dissolves and fades for which the original negative may be needed. It will also save time when the final edited cutting print is matched to the master materials. I have spoken in terms of negative, but this applies equally to the colour master, when you are dealing with 16 mm. colour materials.

Rough Assembly

The main purpose of the first rough assembly is to put the shots which have been photographed in the order dictated by the script. At this stage no attempt should be made to cut the shots to length or to edit them for effect. The object is to see first of all if they will go together in the right order, smoothly and without jarring the action.

With negative checked and numbered, you can really get down to making your first rough assembly. Look first at the script and at any notes made at the viewing of the rushes. Shot one appears to be unaltered, so you look for it in the trim bin. If you are making a mute first rough assembly, or rough cut as it is more often called, you can work on practically any kind of machine. An animated viewer is quite suitable for this kind of work, as is almost any kind of power-operated editing machine. I personally prefer the viewer for these elementary stages. If you are assembling sync. takes the equipment you use is different: I will discuss this shortly. With shot one in your hand, you can place it in the machine you are using. Run down to the start of the shot, losing the spacing and fogged part of the picture and cutting off the clapper board. If there is action, mark the point where the action begins.

Suppose the scene shows three men in an office talking. Wind through and look at the first part of the action. At the start of the shot they appear to be frozen. Although there is no sound you can almost hear the director calling for silence and then action. Then, they all begin to move. One man picks up a telephone. Another passes the third man a cup of coffee. A secretary appears from out of shot and hands the man at the desk a pile of papers, then she disappears. Where should you cut in?

The script lists this as an office interior over which commentary will eventually be heard. For sound it lists only general office hubbub and gives details of the commentator's words. Have another look at the start of the shot. Wind through it carefully until you have found the exact frame where the action starts. Mark it with your wax pencil and join a leader or a piece of white spacing to it. Allow enough spacing to thread up a projector—about 15 ft will probably suffice—and mark on the front of it the title of the film and the fact that this is the cutting copy. A plain C/C is all that is needed. Then mark "reel 1 ACTION". You will have no difficulty in identifying it. What is far more important, it will not be lost when an absent-minded projectionist puts it in the wrong can and sends it to someone else after a viewing. Always identify everything.

With a leader on the start of the film, you will be able to take up the film on a spool and return to consider the shot which forms the start of the action. You now have to find a place to cut out of the shot. Until commentary has been recorded and laid, you cannot be quite certain where it should be, for obviously you will try to match the action to the requirements of the dialogue as accurately as possible. At this stage, when the work of editing is just beginning, it pays to leave everything rather longer than you really want. It is always easier to trim a shot later when commentary has been recorded, than to find and replace the piece of film you have removed. You may decide later that you want it back again. Sometimes, you are bound to find that a shot needs to be even longer than you antici-pated. The parts of a shot which you do not use should always be replaced in the trim bin after a cut has been made. This does not, of course, apply to material which is obviously useless. Fogged shots, unsteady ones and other misfortunes can be committed to the waste bin. But extra lengths of usable material should be returned to the trim bin. Everyone has his own particular system. I person-ally like to write the shot number and the letter T on the trim before

I actually put it back in the bin. This saves my picking the trim up several times thinking it is another shot, and also makes it as easy as possible to find.

Where to Cut

Let us return again to the scene in the office. At the start there is a sudden burst of activity, then the girl enters and leaves her pile of papers with the man at the desk. She leaves and the hubbub continues for a few frames before the action is stopped. Now where should you cut out? If you cut when the secretary hands over the papers, you may well be wrong. If the director had wanted to cut there, why would he have kept the action going until the girl walked out of shot? Check the script again and see if there is any detailed cutting point listed. Does it say, SECRETARY ENTERS AND PASSES PAPERS TO DIRECTOR. *cut.* SCENE 2. *Int. Day. CU Director takes papers and looks at them*, and so on? Or is the next scene entirely different, filmed perhaps at a different location? If so, and this is an isolated office scene which is not part of a sequence photographed at the same location, you will have more freedom to choose your cutting point. In the example in question, I would suggest waiting until the secretary walks out of shot, rather than cutting in the middle of movement. There are exceptions to this, and in an action sequence particularly, cuts in the middle of movement can be very effective. If you cut where the secretary is half way across the room between the desk and the edge of the shot, you will not be committing a cardinal error. But it is better to wait until she goes out of shot.

There can be no hard and fast rules about where you should cut. With experience, you will find you can sense the right point. Perhaps the second shot you have to assemble shows a lorry standing on the edge of a gravel pit. A bulldozer is shunting to and fro moving large amounts of gravel which it shovels into the back of the lorry. Where should you cut into and out of this kind of shot? Look at it carefully and note the exact movements of the bulldozer. It first of all digs into the pile of gravel, then lifts it up in its mechanical grab. Then it reverses away from the pile, turns round and moves towards the parked lorry. It then tips the gravel into the back of the lorry, before reversing and moving back for the next load. Now, where should you cut? There are several possibilities. The bulldozer lunges into the gravel and shovels it up, then raises its mechanical grab. There is a slight pause when the

75

grab has been hoisted whilst the driver changes gear. He reverses. There is another pause while he again changes gear before advancing to the lorry. When the load has been tipped there is another pause and so on. To cut in any of these pauses would be satisfactory. But before making a cut check the script and make sure what part of the operation the film is supposed to be showing.

Assembly editing is largely a matter of commonsense—a matter of matching the action when cutting from scene to scene. It you have to cut together two shots of someone walking, you will need to take particular care. Make sure first of all that the two shots you are cutting together have been photographed from different camera positions. It is quite acceptable to cut from long shot to mid shot or from mid shot to close up, or indeed from a front view to a profile. It is not, however, acceptable to cut from one shot of a man walking, to another shot of the same man walking if the two shots have been taken from a similar position. A cutaway must first be inserted. Let us first assume that you are cutting from a long shot to a mid shot of one man walking down a street. Where do you cut? The answer, as is the case with so much editing technique, is really a matter of common sense. Look at the action and mark the point where his feet are in a definite position. Perhaps his left foot is flat on the ground, and his right foot is just leaving it. In fact his right toe is bent and his heel is about the same level as the ankle of his left foot. That is on the long shot. Now look at the incoming mid shot and select an identical position. Cut the two together and check them to make sure that the action is smooth and make any adjustment necessary. Do not cut when one foot is in mid air. In the same manner, if later in the sequence he stops and lights a cigarette and you have to cut from mid shot to close up, make the cut before he takes out his lighter and cigarettes. Or, you could cut when he is actually lighting them, with his hand comparatively still, and not when his arm is in mid air between pocket and face. Always match the action when cutting from scene to scene.

Using Cutaways

Sometimes you will not be able to match the action of two comparable shots. Perhaps the scenes have been badly directed or photographed by someone who does not know much about editing. Let us look again at the example of the man walking along a street. Let us assume this time that the script calls for two shots, one

76

showing him entering one end of the street and another showing him leaving the opposite end. No good editor will be able to cut the two scenes together, unless the scenes have been very carefully photographed in a manner which disguises the fact that the man is in fact walking a very long walk in the space of a few seconds. If one end of the street with a man in it, is cut straight on to a shot of the other end of a street with the same man in it, the action will appear extremely unnatural. How do you cope with this kind of problem?

This is an occasion for the use of a cutaway. A cutaway is, in essence, an excuse for either poor continuity or the passing of time. The nature of, and the need for cutaways is best described by giving an example.

Imagine an interview with someone arriving at an airport. The camera is set up facing the person being interviewed. He arrives and the camera records his answers to the questions put before him. The camera remains on him, and him alone. The director, standing beside the camera listens to the answers and realises that he will not want to use part of the answer given to one of the questions. He wants to use the beginning and the end of the man's answer but not the middle of it.

The director knows that, as the camera has not been moved since the start of the interview, to cut the offending sentence will be impossible without jarring the action. If he simply cuts out the words he doesn't like the man being interviewed will appear to jump where the piece of film has been removed. The director knows that sound is being recorded on separate tape. The editor will be editing sound and picture on two separate pieces of film. Accordingly, when the interview is over, the director moves his camera round to concentrate on the man who is asking the questions. The man being interviewed does not feature in the shot. The camera is run, without running the sound equipment, and a silent shot of the interviewer listening is obtained.

Later on when the editor starts his side of the work on this sequence he will be able to cut the dialogue at the point where the man's comments are not wanted. At the same point he will cut the action from the man being questioned to the shot of the interviewer. The remainder of the required dialogue is brought up over the shot of the interviewer. At a convenient point the action is cut back to show the man who is speaking.

The intermediate shot of the interviewer is generally known as a cutaway.

Forms of Cutaway

The cutaway can take many forms. Take the case of a man walking down the length of a street, for example. It would be quite acceptable to cut from a shot of the man entering one end of the street to a shot of someone watching him from a nearby window, and back to him walking towards the opposite end of the street. An

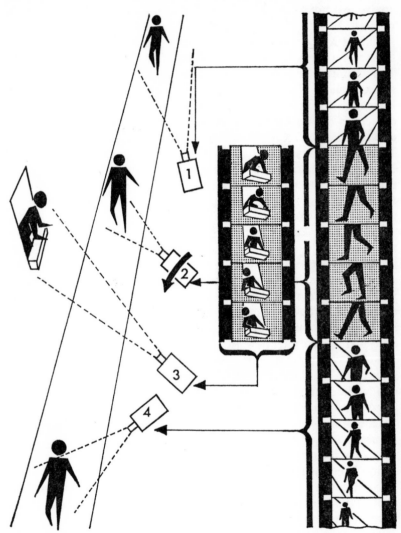

Using cutaways. Camera 1: man enters one end of street. Camera 4: man leaves opposite end of street. Cameras 2 and 3 are possible cutaways.

alternative would be to cut from the first shot to a close-up of his feet walking on the pavement, then back to the street shot. The movements of the feet must be matched on the cut. Also the feet and pavement only must appear in the close-up and none of the surroundings.

The intermediate shots I have suggested distract the audience slightly from the main course of the action and allow an otherwise unacceptable cut to be made without trouble. Cutaways must, of course, always be relevant. It's useless just putting in any old shot you happen to have spare. Choose one which refers to the action in question, and edit it carefully. In the case of the spectator watching the man walking down the street, make sure he or she is looking in the right direction. If in the first shot the man is right off screen, the person in the cutaway must be looking from left to right. Do everything you can to ensure that one shot follows another as smoothly as possible.

Let us consider some further examples. Consider a sequence showing the loading of equipment on a ship. The purpose of the sequence is to show how a new car was loaded into a ship's hold. First of all the car was driven on to a wooden platform which was immediately hoisted up by crane and swung out over the open hold of the ship. In the normal course of events, car and platform would have been lowered straight down to the hold but, when the cameraman was filming this scene, the crane driver had some technical trouble and there was quite a long pause between the car reaching the top of the hold and being lowered down into it. The cameraman therefore stopped filming. When he heard the crane motor starting again, he restarted his camera and filmed the car being lowered into the hold. Unfortunately he photographed the second part of the action from exactly the same position as the first and, when the two exposures were spliced together the action appeared to jump unnaturally. A cut like this is known as a jump cut. To avoid this effect, you should use a cutaway. Mark the point where the crane stops turning and the car is suspended over the open ship's hold. That is the point to insert the cutaway. The cameraman, if he knows what he is doing, will have provided a number of cutaways to choose from. He may perhaps have shot a view of the crane driver sitting in his cab, controlling the crane's movement. Alternatively, he may have shot down into the hold showing the dockers waiting in the hold looking up towards the camera. There are many possibilities. Insert one of these cutaways, and then cut back to the shot at a point just before the crane lowers the car into the hold.

The action should then appear smooth and natural and there will be no unnecessary delays.

In the case of an aircraft landing, it is often necessary to condense the time between touch down and the passengers alighting and moving into the customs hall. Here again a straight cut from one scene to the other will not normally be acceptable. Time must be allowed for the aircraft to pass along the runway and across the tarmac to the customs hall. Shots of people watching the arrival from a passenger building, or of officials moving a gangway into position are typical of the sort of shot which can be used as a cutaway.

Working without Cutaways

Sometimes you will find the cameraman just hasn't filmed any cutaways. This is a rather more difficult problem. You still have a glaring continuity error, but you do not have an obvious cure for it. In this case there are two alternative solutions. Let us return again to the aircraft arrival scene. If the cameraman has had the good sense to let the aeroplane pass out of shot in the first exposure (the actual landing) he may also have been wise enough to start his camera before the plane comes into shot in front of the customs hall. In a case like this you could, as a last resort, cut from one to the other, making sure that the plane was actually out of shot when the cut was made. Sound, skilfully laid and mixed at a later date would do something to smooth out the rather poor continuity. A far better remedy would be to dissolve or "mix" from one shot to the other. This kind of effect is known as an optical. The ways in which opticals are used are discussed later.

So you continue with your first rough assembly. Sometimes you will find that the shot called for in the script is missing. Perhaps it has not yet been shot, or perhaps the director has planned to use a library stock shot at this particular point. Later on you will have to find this material and cut it in. For the first rough cut, however, you can simply build the shot up with spacing marking on it the appropriate scene number and the words *scene missing*.

Matching Action in Cuts

Sometimes you have to cut a sequence of shots filmed on the same set or location.

If you are cutting together more than one view of the same subject you must take very great care to match the outgoing and incoming actions precisely.

Here is a scene where three people are eating in a restaurant. This will serve as an example of the technique. But let us first look at the script and see exactly what the three shots to be cut together contain.

Scene 1: Int. Restaurant Day. LS. Three people sit at table eating. We see there is one man and his wife and young son. The son is looking eagerly at a waiter who approaches the table with an ice-cream.

CUT

Scene 2: Int. Restaurant Day. CMS. The waiter hands the boy the ice-cream. The boy takes it and drops it on the table cloth.

CUT

Scene 3: Int. Restaurant Day. CU. The boy tries to scoop up the ice-cream with his spoon, hoping his father has not noticed that he has spilled it.

In these three simple shots we have every opportunity to make a series of continuity errors. When putting shots one and two together, care must be taken to match the action exactly. Note where the ice-cream is in relation to both the waiter and the small boy at the end of the first shot, and find the corresponding position in the incoming exposure. Now look for a place where the action is the same and where there is a minimum of movement. Are they holding the ice-cream with their hands in the same position? Is the small boy looking down or up? Are all the points at the end of the first shot the same as those at the beginning of the second one? If you are sure they are not different, cut the scenes together and run through until you find a suitable point to cut to the third exposure.

A cut tends to make the action in a sequence more noticeable. As the boy drops the ice-cream, a cut would tend to slightly emphasise his nervousness. It may be possible to hold the second shot until he has actually dropped the ice-cream and looked up to see if his father has noticed. This would be quite a good thing to do. Then cut to the close-up. By cutting at that point you are emphasising the boy's reaction and reminding the audience that he is worried in case anyone else has noticed. Match the angle of his head, the position of the ice-cream and all the other small items. Make sure that if he has his mouth open at the end of the outgoing shot it is open at the point you cut to the new one. When you are sure that the action is the same, make your cut. The three shots would then seem to go together naturally.

The same principle holds good for almost every situation. If you are showing shots in a factory of someone working at a lathe, you must match the action at the start and end of each shot forming part of a sequence. If the man is seen working on the same lathe in consecutive shots, the action must be matched exactly, or a cut-away must be inserted. Cut from long shot to close-up, from mid-shot to close-up or any alternative shot where the perspective is different. If the man has one hand on the controls in the mid-shot make sure it is still there in the close-up. If he is looking ahead of him in the first shot, do not let him look down when you cut to the second view or his head will appear to jump.

The editing of action is not really complicated. It is simply a matter of common sense and observation. With a little care, the first rough cut can run quite smoothly.

At the end of the first rough cut you should have everything in the right running order. Many of the scenes will be considerably over length, but the basic materials for further work will be there. Some shots may be missing. Perhaps they are to be photographed later, or perhaps no plans have been made for the cameraman to shoot them. In these cases you will have to use stock shots of library material.

Missing Shots—Library Material

Most libraries hold quite a wide range of general materials. Long shots and more detailed views of large cities and country scenes, and well-known people and places are usually available from libraries. Many unexpected things can be found there as well. In a London library one would expect to find a number of views of the Houses of Parliament and on a recent search I was not disappointed. I was, however, rather more surprised to find a good shot of a team of musicians playing to a crowd outside a large London store. Libraries come up with even more surprising material.

In every main film production company you will find a library of some kind. A number of independent organisations also exist solely to supply still and ciné library materials. Some of these libraries have another function. If you cannot go abroad to film general background shots for a particular production, the library will possibly be able to get the material for you. They may themselves have the shots you want. Alternatively they may have contacts who can produce the required material from the country concerned.

Fees and Royalties

The library will soon let you know if they feel they have anything of interest. Before you use any library material, find out how much it is going to cost and above all, make sure the copyright is owned by the person who is selling it to you. The next step is for you to go to see what material they can offer. Normally a small search fee is charged for finding the material, and a viewing machine or cinema is provided where prints of the shots they have selected can be viewed. If they have the kind of scene you are looking for, you will be able to order a copy of the shot in question. You will be charged all laboratory costs and a royalty fee. This is usually at a fixed amount per foot of film. When the film is finally edited, measure the amount of each shot you use and let the library have the details. Different royalties apply for each type of audience to which the finished film is to be shown. A film intended for showing to a factory's own employees will therefore probably cost only a matter of shillings. If the same shot is to be incorporated in a film for the cinema or television, this cost will be considerably increased. If the film is to be released all over the world the costs are likely to be even higher. Films for advertising are the most expensive of all.

Libraries may sometimes seem rather too expensive. But if you work out the cost of shooting some of the scenes they provide you will find that the charges are not unreasonable. A simple shot like a general view of London Airport can be quite expensive when you have first of all paid for permission to film there, and then met the cost of film stock, processing and the camera crew to photograph it. A library shot can save time and money. But don't overdo it. Always use library shots which are not already familiar. There are unfortunately plenty of clichés. And don't just use a library shot simply because you have ordered it. Make sure it really is wanted and does contribute something to the sequence it is used in.

Ordering Library Shots

The first step to take if you need anything from a library is to write and tell the librarian exactly what you want. Let him know the name and nature of your production and give him the basic details of the shot you require. Tell him the date of the material you are looking for. This is important. It is absolutely useless asking for stock shots of Trafalgar Square and then trying to cut the scenes any librarian would normally provide to a present-day request, into a film dealing with London in the early 1900s. However, if you want material on Trafalgar Square in 1900, say so, and you may well find the libraries have got it. This may sound stupid advice, but a number of film makers tend to complain that they cannot get material when the real problem is that they simply have not given enough details of what they are looking for.

You must then decide what kind of film stock you wish the library to provide. In the case of a black and white stock shot, the normal procedure is for the library to provide either a fine grain or a duplicate negative. This is all very well in the case of 16 mm. material intended for use with a 16 mm. production, but care must be taken when ordering 35 mm. material for use in a 16 mm. production.

When 35 mm. film is reduced to 16 mm. size the emulsion position of the film is changed. A contact type 35 mm. original will be turned round S.M.P.E. when it is reduced to 16 mm., unless adjustments are made when the material is reduced. For this reason I always prefer to ask for a 35 mm. fine grain from which I can arrange for a suitable 16 mm. contact type dupe negative to be produced.

With colour materials, you can either ask for a duplicate colour master in the case of 16 mm. colour originals or for a 35 mm. inter-positive or inter-negative in the case of film originally shot on 35 mm.

Inter-positive is simply a name given to fine grain prints of colour materials and inter-negative is another way of saying duplicate negative.

At what stage of editing should you order library material? There is no set rule to obey, although there is usually an ultimate deadline to meet. When your edited print is matched to the original material the negative or duplicate colour master of your library material will be needed in the course of completing the work. If you want to see the results on a screen you will have to order a print from your duplicate materials and the print can then be edited into the cutting copy.

You can thus order your library material at any time provided it is ready in time to cut into the final edited version negative or colour master.

It is wise to leave a margin of time in case problems arise in the course of making the duplicate materials.

Damaged Stock Shots

Some stock shots will be in a poor state of repair. Fortunately most libraries are very good at looking after materials entrusted to their care. Sometimes, however, you may need to use a shot provided by some person or organisation not really professionally film minded. It is quite possible that the shot they provide will be either scratched or dirty and as much damage as possible must be repaired before the shot is incorporated in your finished production.

First of all clean the master material. It is absolutely useless trying to do anything with a duplicate in which all the faults of the original have been copied. You must go to the original and, with immense care, clean it with a dry anti-static cloth, or one which has been moistened with carbon tetrachloride. If you hold the film at an angle to the light you will then be able to see any scratches. If the scratches are on the emulsion side, there is little you can do to remedy them. At best you can clean them up a bit and possibly make them rather less noticeable. If, however, they are on the cellulose side of the film, they can very possibly be removed. There are a number of chemical processes which can give good results. Many laboratories will also be able to polish the offending scratch, until it is not noticeable. All this is well worth doing if you want to obtain the best possible quality from library material.

Using Old Film

If you ever need to use really old film materials you are faced with an additional problem. Film shot years ago was photographed at an entirely different speed. Many early cameras were, of course, hand cranked, and the movement and exposure on many old shots is a long way from the standards nowadays required. Old film shown on present-day machines at sound speed tends to look jerky and unevenly exposed, but there is a way of remedying this fault. It is known as stretch printing.

When a film is stretch printed, every second frame is printed twice. This does much to smooth out the jerkiness of action, and in cases of extreme difference, the printer light can be adjusted to compensate for irregular exposure. If you have to use old film in one of your productions you will probably want to have it stretch printed.

If you are using library material, you will not be able to have the original but will have to make do with a duplicate. Make sure this is stretch printed. If you are, however, lucky enough to obtain the original material you will still have to use a duplicate in your final edited version. If you intercut an ordinary dupe of the old material with the new material specially photographed for the production, the laboratory will print both as they stand—for projection at present-day sound speeds. They cannot stretch print part of a reel. You must first have the material you want stretch printed, and then cut the stretch-printed duplicate into the edited material. The laboratory can produce further prints for you from this.

If you are using library material, and you are supplied with an old speed fine grain film, ask the laboratory to stretch print a duplicate negative for you. They can make a print for editing from this, and you will be able to cut the negative into the edited final version of your picture.

Disadvantages of Library Material

There are two main kinds of occasion when stock shots are useful. The first of these occasions is when the material needed cannot be obtained in any other way, as is the case with newsfilm and much historical material.

The second occasion is when the cost of photographing the required shot is not justified for it would cost more to send a camera team out to shoot the shot again than it would to include a library exposure. The first reason is a good one but, in my opinion, the second reason is often used as an excuse.

Many original views of well-known landmarks can still be obtained yet too often editors persist in using the same old library exposures. Think, for example, of the number of times Big Ben and the London Houses of Parliament have been included in films. How many of these occasions has the shot used been the same library view looking over the river with a few boats floating on the Thames in the foreground. No doubt the shot serves its purpose. It identifies the location clearly. Where the film cannot justify the cost of sending a cameraman out to the Houses of Parliament the library shot will save the situation. But if the cost can be met it most certainly should be. There are many new views of the Houses of Parliament which would be far more interesting to an audience.

There are further disadvantages with using library material. I have already outlined the main procedure of ordering material from a library. You will have noticed that the library will never part with the original material. You always get a copy, and often that copy is made from a duplicate master. Definition and picture quality suffer as material gets further and further away from the original. Think of the stages a simple shot goes through before it is seen on the screen as part of your film.

A cameraman first photographs a view of the House of Commons. He shoots on negative which he has processed and sells to the library. They make a fine grain print and from that make another negative. The original is already two stages away. When you order the shot for your film they print their duplicate negative on a fine grain positive stock. You then have a 16 mm. reduction dupe negative made for use in the edited negative of your film. You are now four stages away from the original. The actual print your audience sees will be five generations away from the cameraman's original. Grain and picture sharpness will have suffered considerably. If quality is your first consideration you will do well to keep library material to a minimum.

6

FINE EDITING TECHNIQUE

THE editing of sound and picture go very closely together, especially when you are trying to achieve a particular mood or atmosphere in a film or a sequence. But the pace of a film is governed by the action in the story which in turn suggests to the editor how it should be cut. Generally speaking, slow cutting from scene to scene tends to create a rather more relaxed atmosphere than cutting together a series of short scenes quickly one after the other. Sound and changes of sound tend to emphasise a change in mood. By cutting slowly from scene to scene to start with, and gradually increasing the pace by making each shot slightly shorter than the one which precedes it, tension can be gradually increased. Consider for example scenes of a police car chasing a motor-bicycle through the streets of a big city. At the start of the chase you may have a long shot of the motor-bike roaring away, followed by the police car. Perhaps the shot is held for five seconds. A second shot, showing only the motor-cycle could again be held for five seconds, as could a third shot showing only the car. Cut then to the motor-cycle—holding the shot for five seconds. The motor-cyclist looks over his shoulder at the police car and as he turns you cut to a shot of the car. You hold that for only three seconds before cutting back to the motor-cycle. Tension is increasing. Give three seconds more on the motor-cycle, then a shot of the man riding it, held only for two seconds. A shot of the motor-cycle approaching traffic lights, held for three seconds. The lights changing to red is the subject of a two-second close-up. The cycle skids—again shown in two seconds. In two more seconds the police car skids to a halt. We cut to a longer shot as the police-men get out. This shot is held for four seconds. A longer shot still shows them walk over to the motor-cyclist trapped under his machine. This shot is held for five seconds, and we are back where we started. The tension is over. It started where the chase started, and ended when the motor-cycle skidded. As it grew more tense the scenes followed each other more quickly and the drama of the situation was thus increased.

Shot Length and Pace

The length of time you hold each shot can be used to emphasise a particular point or situation. In a conversation, to give one of many examples, if you are intercutting shots of two people involved in the conversation and want to emphasise one person more than the other, you can do so by holding his or her shot for rather longer than a shot of the other person. Imagine a simple argument, told in five shots. The action each time shows the person who is speaking. The dialogue goes like this:

Shot 1 Man 1: I suppose you think you are clever?
Shot 2 Man 2: Not particularly.
Shot 3 Man 1: Then why did you do it?
Shot 4 Man 2: Because I thought it was necessary.
Shot 5 Man 1: What a silly thing to do.

These shots can be cut together in several different ways. First of all you can keep each shot long, cutting it to a second or so before the dialogue is spoken, and holding it to observe the speaker's immediate reactions. If you do this you will make the situation relatively undramatic, especially if all your shots are of the same length. By making the second and fourth shots shorter than the first, third and fifth you will immediately increase the tension. You will make the first man more aggressive and the exchange will immediately become more interesting. Alternatively you can make the first and second shots of equal length, and hold the third shot for half as long again. "Then why did you do it?" The shot is held for just long enough to stimulate that tiny bit of curiosity and extra interest. If you then cut quickly from the fourth shot to the fifth you will make the first man's summary more emphatic. By altering these cuts in the different ways I have suggested you can slightly emphasise different sides of an argument.

Action Cutting

With action cutting, where you are not concerned with dialogue, there is much more scope for really creative editing.

Let us consider now the building up of tension in another action sequence. The sequence this time deals with the journey of a munitions train through occupied France in the last war. The train contains two carriages of soldiers and much equipment. It is going fast through the night and the driver is unaware that a few miles up the line Resistance workers are mining the track ready to blow up the train when it passes. In the script, the action is intercut between scenes of soldiers getting drunk on the train, the driver coaxing the train to make greater speed, the wheels of the train turning, and Resistance workers wiring fuses several miles up the line. The script simply points out that the scenes have to be cut together. Editing has to make the scene dramatic, for no dialogue is spoken.

Dramatic Situation

It would, of course, be perfectly possible to make all the scenes the same length, but the situation would lack a great deal of drama. It is far better to try to make the scenes more tense by varying the length of the shots as the train nears disaster. Try first of all to understand the dramatic situation. In the train there are two groups of people—soldiers who are not worried about time, and a train driver and his colleague who are. Farther up the line are the Resistance workers, also worried about being caught and very anxious to get the job over before the train comes in sight. With this situation in mind you can form a basic plan of operation. You can decide to make your shots of the soldiers longer than the remainder.

Start with a general outline of the overall position—shots of each of the three main situations, held for round about ten seconds. It would be a good idea to start with the driver and then cut from the soldiers to the Resistance, and then cut back to the train driver again. From the comparatively silent situation two miles up the line, the cut to the noise of the engine will itself have considerable impact. Hold this shot for a shorter period, then go back up the line. This shot again should be shorter than on the previous occasion. Then go back to the soldiers, holding the shot for about the same time. Cut to the train driver, holding for only a few seconds, then back to the Resistance. We can hear the train in the distance now. Back to the driver, and then cut to the train wheels—two very short shots. Cut to the Resistance. Hold for about the same length as the two previous shots put together, then go back to the driver. Hold for the same length. Cut to the deserted line where the Resistance have laid their charges, and hold the shot for only three seconds. The train wheels for three, the driver for three, and then the explosion. Hold the following shots for as long as is necessary. The tension is over.

There are, of course, many ways in which you can assemble a scene of this nature. I have suggested one of them—others may well be much better. But the one I have given will at least show how altering the length of each shot can lend drama to, and shift emphasis from, any situation. This is the whole essence of successful editing. The examples I have given have been of dramatic situations but the principles they illustrate apply equally well to film shot by any factory film unit anywhere. Leave all your shots the same length, and the audience will fall asleep before the film finishes. Vary the tempo and you will keep them interested from beginning to end. Even a machine has its own kind of tempo. Study its movements, and work out your shots and cuts accordingly. You will find the time is well spent and the discoveries you make will not be disappointing.

In the foregoing example we changed from scene to scene by means of a cut. There are several ways of moving from one shot or sequence to another. If you do not want to cut directly from one shot to the next you can gradually merge the two scenes until one replaces the other. The first shot dissolves to the second and for a moment the action becomes a mixture of both shots before becoming only the second shot. This method of transition is called simply dissolving, or more often in television, mixing, from one scene to another. Alternatively you can fade out the first shot and fade in the second, with a brief period of blackness in between the two exposures. These effects, which can take many forms, are known as optical effects.

Using Opticals

Traditionally, dissolves were used to denote the passing of time. If shot two was supposed to take place some time after shot one, the editor would arrange to dissolve from one scene to the other. Nowadays this doctrine is often disregarded and a straight cut is sometimes made, care being taken to ensure that the scene is different enough to avoid the jarring effect caused by cutting two similar scenes together.

Sometimes editors use a dissolve because they simply cannot cut two shots together without a jump in the action. Perhaps the scene has been badly directed or photographed, and there is a pause in the action after which, without a change of scene, the action is started again. To cut the two pieces of action together by simply removing the part of the scene where nothing is happening would make an unacceptable cut and the editor must therefore either find a cutaway, or dissolve from the first piece of action to the second. But, although a dissolve here is useful and better than a jump cut, it is not really the correct use of the optical in question.

Dissolves, like cuts, can contribute to the pace of the action. A cut brings an immediate change of scene and, possibly subconsciously, an immediate audience reaction. A dissolve brings a gradual transition; it can be very gradual if the dissolve is a long one. This alone suggests a time when it is better to mix from scene to scene than to cut. In a slow, dreamy sequence a few mixes will be more suitable than cuts.

Making a film is, in some respects, like writing a book. The film is not divided into chapters and paragraphs but into main and subsidiary sequences. In a book you have punctuation marks and in a film you must also dictate the pace of the proceedings. Dissolves might be considered to mark the end of paragraphs, and fade outs make excellent full stops at the end of chapters.

When to Mix

There can be no definite rules about when to mix from one scene to the next. A change of location can sometimes call for a dissolve from one location to the other. Generally speaking, if you are moving from a location to one which is entirely different either in character or situation a dissolve would be the best way. That is, of course, unless you want to make the difference particularly noticeable, when a straight cut from one scene to the other would emphasise the point. If, for example, you are going to move from an office scene to a shot of people dancing on the floor of a ballroom, it would often be better to dissolve from one scene to the other. The music to which the people are dancing could then be faded up as the dissolve makes one shot merge with the other. A straight cut would be less suitable. If you have to pass from a shot of people sunbathing on the beaches of England to a general seaside view in the South of France, a dissolve might be the best way of moving from one scene to the next. If scenes are similar, yet not identical, a dissolve is often the best thing to use. There are other occasions, however.

If one particular character appears in two following shots one of which is seen immediately after the other, you may well be able to move from scene to scene with a cut provided, as I have already explained, the actions can be matched at the point at which the cut is made. Perhaps, however, the action cannot be matched, or is deliberately different. In one scene perhaps we see a man working in a factory and in the very next scene we see the same man sun-bathing on the shore. To cut directly from one scene to the other with the same man in view on both occasions would be entirely wrong. You should dissolve from one scene to the other. This applies when the man is himself visible throughout both exposures. If he is visible throughout the first shot and only in the latter part of the seashore exposure, you may well be able to move from one to the other with a cut. Perhaps the sea scene starts with a general view of the beach showing thousands of people, before the camera pans round to show the man in question soaking up the sun. In a case like that you would be fully justified in cutting from the pre-ceding office scene to that taking place at the seaside. The general view of many people would be acting as a cutaway. You would not therefore, technically, be cutting directly from one shot of a man at one location to another of the same man at an entirely different location. When such changes of scene are quite inevitable use either a cutaway or a dissolve.

Dissolves may still be used in the traditional way to denote the passing of time. In its simplest form the dissolve can be used to mix from shots of a calendar showing the month of January, to a view of the same calendar showing the page for December. You cannot directly cut from one shot to the other if the camera's observation point is the same and if the audience is expected to believe that one complete year has passed. A dissolve must be used. If you are moving from a day scene to a night one a dissolve can often be used. Here again, if the location is the same in two consecutive exposures, a dissolve must link them, for a cut would be totally unsuitable.

Sometimes you may not need to use a dissolve at all. You may just wish to use it for effect. Dissolves, when carefully prepared, can be very effective, but to ensure the best possible result both exposures must be carefully matched. Scenes which are similar in pictorial composition can often make particularly pleasing dissolves, for one scene appears to become the other with the minimum of varia-tion in density and texture. There are thousands of possible uses for dissolves in almost any kind of film making and experiment is well worth while.

A dissolve or mix is not the only way of moving from one scene to another. The wipe is another accepted method of transition. In a wipe one scene is moved horizontally in one direction and another scene is introduced immediately behind it. The change can be from left to right of screen or from right to left. This method is much favoured by newsreel producers.

7

PRODUCING A SOUNDTRACK

IN an earlier chapter I stressed the importance of supplying full and interesting soundtrack material to the editor. Let us now examine the stages by which that soundtrack is produced. The objective in producing a soundtrack is to mould into one homogeneous sequence the various effects, music and commentary recordings which complement the visuals. This is the detailed final mixed soundtrack that the audience will hear. How does this soundtrack originate? Here is a brief summary of the main stages in soundtrack production. We will follow this in greater detail later.

The first step to take is to view the edited picture. You can't really begin to add music or sound effects until you have almost finished editing your picture. If you start before, and begin to build up the different soundtracks, you will find that every time you alter a cut in the picture you have to make the same cut at the same point in all your different soundtracks. This could involve you in many complications and a great amount of extra work. Edit your picture and synchronised dialogue to begin with, and then think about other sounds. Now, look at the picture and make notes of everything you need. Then gather together the materials you have listed. You will find you have some music and sound effects on film, some on tape and probably some on gramophone records. Before you can use any of these they will have to be transferred to the right gauge of sprocketed magnetic film.

Breaking Down Sound Film

When you have had your sound transferred you will have before you a reel of edited picture and a variety of different sounds on sprocketed film. The next thing to do is to break down the newly recorded soundtracks. The term sounds destructive. But breaking down film reels simply means separating the different sounds from each other. The normal way to do this is to run through each reel of sound on either a synchroniser with track reader or an editing machine. Break off each piece of film containing a sound effect at the end of that particular recording. Then rewind the pieces you have detached, each on its own separate roll. In the end the few big reels of sound you had will have been divided into a larger number of little ones, each containing one kind of sound. Label each roll carefully so that you can find it in a hurry if need be.

Building Tracks for Mix

Now you can return to the edited picture and start adding your sound. If shot one shows a scene in a city and shot two shows a scene somewhere in the country you look for two of the effects you are planning to use for these scenes. Perhaps you have a background traffic roar for the city and a country atmosphere track for the other view. Using a synchroniser put the piece of traffic sound opposite the picture of the city scene. Make sure that the sound starts at the same time as the picture. If, however, you want it faded up, it should be started several feet before the picture begins. And cut it level with the picture at the other end, unless you want the sound mixer to blend the city traffic with the sound of the incoming scene. You are now using two parts of the synchroniser. In the front you have your reel of picture and, in the next track you have your city sound. Now in the track behind that place your country atmosphere soundtrack alongside the picture to which it refers. Where the city scene ends and the country scene begins you will want to lose your traffic soundtrack. Thus you splice white leader on to the end of that particular effect track at the end of the scene to which it refers. Likewise you will not want the country sounds over the shot of the city so the first part of your second soundtrack can be built up with spacing material. How does the assembly look if you wind through the reel so far? At the beginning, on all three parts of the synchroniser you will find a piece of leader. The start of a reel must always be identified with a leader. Winding on you come to the first scene—the city. At the same point as the city scene cuts in on the picture, the sound for it cuts in on the first of the soundtracks. Meanwhile, spacing continues on the other soundtrack. At the end of that scene the countryside picture begins. At the same point the first soundtrack is spliced to spacing and the spacing on the second soundtrack is spliced to an incoming

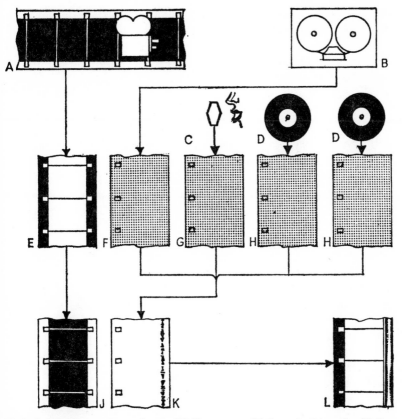

Method of building up a soundtrack. (A) Shoot mute. (B) Record wild tracks. (E) Process camera original and edit print from it. (C) Record commentary and edit to picture. (D and E) Add sound effects and music from tape and disc on separate tracks. (F) Transfer wild tracks to perforated magnetic for editing. Mix all tracks together in dubbing theatre and transfer final mix to optical sound negative (K). Print optical sound negative with edited mute camera original (J) together on positive stock (L).

soundtrack of countryside atmosphere. Build up the backgrounds first. These are the first stages in sound editing.

After that you can go through again and, without altering your background tracks, add some more. These, too, must exactly match the edited picture. Using these tracks you can add any special details you want in the scenes. Perhaps a bus passes in the foreground. This can be laid on another track whilst people talking and walking could be added on another, and so on. When you have finally built up all the soundtracks you need, run through them and make out a dubbing cue sheet. This is a sheet to guide the sound mixer. It contains a list of all soundtracks and effects. It also gives the precise footages at which you want them to start or end when they are all mixed together to make one track.

With the tracks and cue sheets go into a dubbing theatre and mix your tracks together. You have then finished editing the sound.

Editing Synchronised Takes

If you are only handling sequences of synchronised sound you will have few editing problems. Once the rushes have been synchronised all you have to do is to put the scenes together in the right order in the most suitable place. An editing machine and a synchroniser with track reader will be most useful for this. First remove the clapper board from the first shot and join on a leader. Now you can run through to the first cutting point. If the script calls for a level cut you can make the cut on an editing machine.

A level cut[1] is one where sound and picture are cut at the same point. If, for example, an interviewer is asking someone a question, you can cut from the interviewer to the person who is going to answer the question at almost any point. If the action starts with a shot of the interviewer, with his voice on the soundtrack, you can wait until he finishes speaking. Then cut from his picture and his soundtrack, to show the person who is answering and hear his comments. Such a cut would be a level cut because sound and picture are cut at the same point.

Laid Sound

The sound and picture do not have to cut across at the same point. If you wish you can cut from the picture of the interviewer to the picture of the person who will answer, before he has finished asking his question. Then you will find the cut easier to make on a synchroniser. You simply put the first shot in the synchroniser with sound and picture and wind on to the point where you wish to cut from one view to the other. Mark the action here with a wax pencil.

In another part of the synchroniser you now place the second shot with its soundtrack, taking care that the soundtrack comes in after the other one has ended. Mark the points where you are to join the two soundtracks, then wind back to the mark you have already made on the outgoing picture. Make a similar mark on the incoming action, and cut across. Sound and picture will still be in

[1] *U.S. term "straight cut" or "editorial cut".*

98

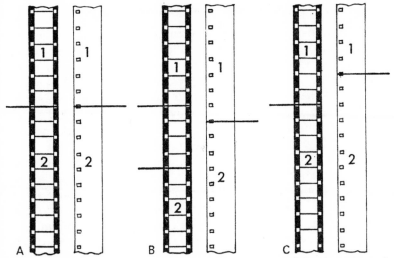

When editing a synchronised interview it is possible to cut sound and picture at the same point (A) or to cut the sound under cover of a cutaway (B) or to overlay part of the track (C).

sync. The only difference is that when projected, the action will now change from a shot of the interviewer to the other person rather earlier than before. The interviewer's voice will continue over the second shot. A voice carried over in this manner is said to be *laid*.

This technique is rather useful to emphasise a particular point. Cuts give emphasis. So if you want to emphasise a particular part of the question, a cut in the picture before the point you wish to outline will make it more noticeable.

The editing of synchronised dialogue is not really difficult. Any kind of interview can be edited in a synchroniser. Mark before you cut and you won't have any trouble. These comments do, of course, apply only to editing film with a separate magnetic soundtrack.

In this connection the use of cutaway shots for synchronised takes is again worth mentioning. You can cut away at any point and, with the aid of a synchroniser, the whole operation only takes a few seconds. Mark the point where you wish to cut out of your original exposure and the point where you want to come back to it. Put the shot you are going to use as a cutaway in one of the other tracks of the synchroniser and make corresponding marks. Join the film at the appropriate marks, being sure to make your cut and your splice on the left of the synchroniser to preserve synchronisation. The track can be carried through without a cut.

Uneven and Missing Soundtracks

When editing sync. takes you often find that the sound level of different recorded takes is slightly different. Background noise may also vary considerably. Consider for example a series of interviews taking place in a busy street. The volume of traffic will never be the same at the end of one interview and at the start of another. Any cut made in the track at the end of the dialogue will therefore need improvement. To overcome this, further soundtracks must be added and the different tracks mixed together.

Some films, as I have already pointed out, are photographed without any synchronised sound. Others have some sync. takes and a number of other silent ones. In cases like this, where only part of the film is shot with synchronised sound, the sync. tracks must, in editing, be built up with spacing so that synchronisation is preserved. If, again for the sake of an example, the film starts and ends with a synchronised dialogue sequence, the end of the first sequence is joined on to spacing. The spacing is then carried through to the start of the last sequence where the incoming magnetic track must be joined. Both interviews will then be in synchronisation with the action to which they refer from the start of the reel. Sound for the intervening scenes will have to be provided, and it is then that editing really becomes an interesting task.

Ordering Sound Effects

First you must collect the necessary raw materials. Apart from synchronised dialogue, you will be concerned with three main kinds of additional sound. Commentary is the first of the three, music the second, and sound effects the third. All three are vital to the success of any film, although music is perhaps the most dispensable for some kinds of production. A film with commentary alone will quickly become boring. A film with sound effects alone or with music from beginning to end may need some kind of explanation even if it is only an introduction or summary.

In the course of production the film unit may have recorded a number of wild tracks. These are probably sound effects, but could possibly include *un*synchronised dialogue, perhaps for use in a crowd scene or some similar gathering where dialogue needs to be audible over background hubbub. Other sound effects are, of course, needed and you will have to either arrange for them to be specially recorded or obtain them from sound effects libraries which may have suitable recordings on disc or on tape.

100

Start by winding through the cutting copy and work out the sound effects you need. Make a list, and be sure it is a detailed one. List precisely the effects you require, and note the length of the shots so you can calculate how much you want to use.

The need to be precise cannot be over-emphasised. I once met someone who had telephoned a sound effects library and asked for a church bell recording to be delivered. A hundred and fifty records were sent to him and he found himself half buried in recordings of bells of every kind from small country churches to Italian cathedrals! He should, of course, have stated that he wanted a church bell for use with a church in a county town centre.

This need to specify exactly what you want applies equally well to all kinds of sound effect. It is quite useless simply asking for a car effect. You must be much more specific. Is it a sports car or a saloon? What is the make and approximate year of manufacture? Is it going forwards or backwards and at what speed? Is there a visible gear change in the course of the shot? Does the shot include someone switching on and starting the engine or someone braking and turning it off? These are only a few of the questions you must ask yourself before ordering sound effects. If you think it is all unnecessary, listen to a soundtrack of a modern sports car over picture of a modern saloon and see how absurd the sound is. That is an exaggerated example, but it is very easy to make far more subtle mistakes. Perhaps you are not an expert on cars, but try to get it right because someone in the audience probably is.

And, when you look at the cutting copy, think carefully of all the effects you will need for each shot. A good soundtrack is made up of a number of different sound effects. Take, for example, a shot of traffic passing through a main thoroughfare. The shot includes views of three cars and a bus passing the camera. To complete this soundtrack correctly, the sound of these cars and the bus must be reconstructed on the soundtrack. Behind them, you will need a background atmosphere track of the general hubbub of the main road. A further track with a few motor horns could be added to give extra detail, and a newsvendor's voice would add a little more realism. These effects are all needed if you want to build up a perfect soundtrack.

When you have chosen the main effects, concentrate on the detailed ones. Look at the footsteps of leading characters appearing in the action. These, too, should be audible and suitable sound to use must be recorded. These sounds can be obtained from sound libraries, or recorded specially for the production in question. Note the kind of surface the character is walking on. If it is a hard stone surface or a pavement the sound will be different from a gravel path or lino.

There are several ways of reproducing footsteps. Time permitting, it is far better to record them at the time of shooting and then match them to the action in the course of editing. Alternatively, they can be done *live* to picture. This is where the action is followed on the screen and the effect is manufactured in the studio to fit it. However, you need to be an expert to achieve acceptable results without wasting a great deal of time. Other effects like cups being placed on tables, and cigarette lighters can be done live to picture in a suitable recording theatre, but here again, it is better to list the required sounds and shoot them wild, then match the effect to the action. Effects of this kind, when done live to picture, are known as *spot effects*.

Cheated Sound Effects

Sometimes you will not be able to find the exact effect you are looking for. You may then be forced by lack of time or money to find some alternative. Occasionally you may find something better than you were originally looking for.

I remember spending a considerable amount of time trying to find a suitable effect for a mechanical hoist, used at the end of a car factory assembly line to lower the finished car bodies on to the chassis. I listened to every crane and electric motor effect I could obtain and found them all unsatisfactory. Then I came across a recording of an ordinary household food mixer. It was a record which was designed to be played at 78 rpm. I played it at 45 rpm and the effect was exactly what I wanted. It has been my favourite mechanical hoist ever since!

On another occasion I wanted to reproduce the noise of gravel being tipped into an empty lorry. There are, of course, hundreds of good recordings of this effect, but at that time I hadn't got one of them. As the film was wanted in a hurry I had to pick up the sound from other materials. I actually used a recording of the Niagara Falls, again playing it at the wrong speed, and fading it up and down as the gravel was tipped in and as the lorry filled to capacity. It sounded splendid!

When you are choosing your sound effects, think not only of the obvious ones, but of those less evident. Even if a particular sound cannot be directly connected with anything visible in the picture, it can lend much to the atmosphere of a scene. Shots of a pond call for some kind of exterior atmosphere, but the scene is greatly enhanced with a few suitable bird noises. A distant train has often been used to suggest character to a scene. There is really no such thing as complete silence. Every location has its own atmosphere and even in a carpeted room rustles of clothing can be easily heard. Anyone who doubts the value of sound should make an effort to see *Listen to Britain*, a wartime documentary which, although rather slow by present-day standards, conveys its message almost entirely by using authentic sounds.

Selecting Music

In addition to sound effects you will also need music. If the choice of music is left to you, choose something which is really suitable. Check the copyright—make certain before you use it that it is clearable for the areas in which you want to show the finished film. Be sure, too, that it is clearable at a price the producers of the film can afford. This is by no means always the case. Again the cost of clearing music, like that of using library material, is assessed by considering the amount of music used and the type of audience the finished film is to be shown to.

Perhaps you do not want to use classical or popular music recorded by companies marketing their records through the usual outlets. You may decide to use mood recordings produced by companies specialising in the production of recordings which are internationally clearable and which are designed for film and television users. Most mood music publishers can provide a catalogue listing the tapes and discs they are able to supply. They are normally classified by types of music and the variety of different kinds available is quite astonishing.

Anyone wanting a thirty-second piece of music to add dramatic impact to a scene can choose from several hundred different recordings or what are known as *dramatic stings*. Lighthearted curtain raisers and short musical links for every kind of mood are also plentiful and the selection of longer pieces is really enormous. Whatever the instrument, and whatever the nationality, somewhere it is usually possible to obtain a mood music recording.

Study the different publishers' catalogues, and then ask them to supply the recordings you want to hear. You may be charged with the cost of all the records supplied but will only be charged royalties on the recordings you actually use in the finished film.

8

MECHANICS OF EDITING SOUND

Sound Transfers

BEFORE the business of editing begins all your chosen music and sound effects recordings must, first of all, be re-recorded on perforated magnetic film. This material puts the sound in a form that can be handled alongside the visuals. Most dubbing theatres have allied transfer facilities. You can take your records and tapes along and have them transferred to either 16 mm. or 35 mm. magnetic film depending on which you prefer to edit and which your editing machine can cope with. Transfer time is quite expensive. It is worth working out in advance the footages of the tape you want to transfer and the exact part of the disc you want to re-record.

Tell the transfer recordist exactly what you need. Let him know if you want to record on 16 mm. and the speed at which you want to re-record. For most purposes this will be 24 frames per second, but for television in some countries, including Great Britain, 25 f.p.s. is standard. You might think one frame would make no difference, but it does. Listen to any familiar piece of music at 24 f.p.s. and then play the 24 f.p.s. recording at 25 f.p.s. and you will immediately notice the difference.

It is possible to record on one of two positions of a 16 mm. magnetic track. Some tracks consist of centre track recordings—the middle of the film. Others are edge track—on the edge opposite the sprocket holes. There isn't very much to choose between them and you are really best advised to pick whatever is normal local practice. In England centre track is rather more common than edge, but all sound transfer and dubbing theatres are equipped to cope with both types. Editing equipment will also accept tracks of both standards.

On 35 mm. film, it is again possible to have two different tracks—one on each side of the stock and, unlike 16 mm., on 35 mm.

you can use both tracks. It is quite normal to record one track in one direction on one side of the stock and another in the other direction near the opposite set of perforations.

If you cannot yourself attend a transfer session, be sure you send really detailed instructions to guide the recordist. State the speed of the recording you wish to transfer. If it is a disc, tell him which band to re-record and how much of it is wanted, and state whether you are talking about the front or the back of the record. It is no use giving a record number and saying band two. He wants to know what side. Some record companies use the same number for both sides of a recording. If you are sending tape for transfer, again state the speed. Is it full track or half track and at what speed was it recorded?

You should normally transfer rather more sound than is needed to cover the actual scene depicted on the film. When the soundtracks are mixed together in a dubbing theatre, an overlap may be needed to provide smooth transition from one sound to another. In fact it always pays to record more sound than you ever expect to need. Some sounds, of course, do not need to be lifted to the length of the shot. If you have a very long street scene you may need to re-record the actual sounds of any vehicles passing near to the camera. You will also need a background traffic effect of a general roar—but you will not need to record enough of it to cover the whole scene. You should transfer your background sound to magnetic (perforated) film in the normal way. You can then loop a section of the sound you have lifted so the same piece runs round and round throughout the entire scene.

Recording Loops

When recording sound you intend to loop, take care not to record anything which makes it obvious. If you have one outstanding effect it will be noticed every time the loop goes round. In the case of the traffic loop for example avoid any obvious motor horns or voices. And make the loop long enough to avoid being obviously repetitive. All you have to do is to record a length of the effect you want to loop. Pick two points where the recording levels are identical and splice the two points end to end to form a loop. Make sure before you join the ends together that the loop is not twisted. Take care also to splice at a point where there is only background atmosphere, not in the middle of a specific effect where the join will be noticed at once.

Loops can save a great deal of trouble. Their main use is in providing background atmospheres. Conversation loops for theatre scenes, factory noise loops for industry, countryside loops for open air scenes are all useful. The main characteristic of a loop should be overall atmosphere, lacking specific detail of any kind. If you want detail, provide it on your other soundtracks—use a loop to back it up. In the case of a car drawing up in the middle of a field, for example, the car arriving should be laid on one soundtrack. The car doors opening and being shut should be laid on another as should any audible footsteps. A background countryside atmosphere of wind and birds should be supplied by a loop. The same principle applies in a factory. If you are showing a machine, put the actual effect of the machine on a separate soundtrack. Use a background factory atmosphere loop to back it up. You will be surprised how a good loop will improve the authenticity of a scene, and of course it also saves time and stock costs.

Recording a Commentary

Before you can start editing your music and effects and matching them to the action, you will have to obtain and edit the film commentary. Sometimes you may not be able to record it at this stage, for the producers may wish to write it when the film is completely finished and add it live in the course of dubbing. This can be done, but the course is not really recommended.

It is far better to record your commentary at the same time as the music and effects and then adjust the picture to match it exactly. The advantages are numerous. You can be sure that the commentary will be exactly where you want it to be. You will also save time in the dubbing theatre because few commentators get a live commentary right first time. Much time can be lost going back and forth with the picture until the commentator gives the required performance at the right point.

Brief your commentator beforehand and give him the script at least a day before you are due to record it. When he has studied it, listen to what he has to say about it. He may ask for the wording of some passages to be altered slightly. Do not say "No" on principle. He knows what he can read without sounding awkward and, if wording can be altered to suit him without changing the meaning, it is worth making the alteration. Tell him what words you would like him to emphasise and where you want him to pause. Make sure that where there is to be a gap in the film commentary, he pauses for long enough to enable you to cut the track without cutting an echo of his voice or a breath being drawn. If you take these simple precautions you should have no trouble. When the recording session is completed you should have several reels of unedited commentary, music and sound effects. With these in hand you can return to the cutting-room.

Now you are faced with another session breaking down sound material. When you have broken down all the effects you will be able to start editing the sound.

Laying the Commentary Track

Now you will again look at your cutting copy. Taking the first part of the commentary you have recorded, and subsequently broken down into sentences or paragraphs, you thread the picture and sound together on an editing machine. You can now adjust the two until the commentary comes in at the right point. Run back to the start of the commentary and splice on a leader or spacing making sure that some kind of start mark occurs at exactly the same point as the start mark on the picture. When you have tidied up the start of the commentary track in this manner you can again return to the end of the first shot.

Perhaps, now you have the commentary to cover the shot, you will find that in the first rough assembly you have left the action too long. Now is the time to shorten it, until the commentary fits exactly. Perhaps, however, the action proves to be too short. In this case you have two alternatives. You can either extend the spacing on the start of the track so that the commentary starts rather later, or divide the commentary into two parts. This is provided, of course, there is a point where the sentence or sentences can be divided without making nonsense of the dialogue. If there is such a point you simply mark it on the cellulose side of the track with a wax pencil. Making sure you do not lose synchronisation by cutting on the left-hand side of the editing machine (before the gate and not after it), you simply splice spacing on to the track at the end of the first sentence. The spacing can be carried through up to the point where you want the second sentence to begin. Here the second piece of track can be joined to it.

All soundtracks consist of a considerable amount of spacing as well as magnetic sound stock and the practice of building up sound in this manner is quite commonplace. Some sequences may not have any commentary at all. For those you will again need to build up the commentary track with spacing. By this method you ensure that the commentary exactly matches the appropriate scene and remains in perfect synchronisation from one end of the reel to the other.

Checking Commentary Sync.

The building up of a commentary track alongside the edited picture by using spacing in the manner already described is known as laying a commentary track. The commentary track will be the first of several tracks you will have to lay in the course of editing. By the time you have finished laying the commentary you should have a reel of edited picture very near in length to the ultimate length of the film, for in fitting commentary to picture and picture to commentary many adjustments will have to be made. When you have finished the track, it is well worth winding back to the start of the reel and then projecting it again. Watch each cut carefully to make sure it is still acceptable. Check the action and the commentary against the script to make sure that they are exactly what is required. When you are sure it is right, put the commentary away in a can and rewind the action.

Splices on Magnetic Track

When splicing spacing to magnetic sound it is worth noting that the type of splice required is slightly different from that normally required when joining two pieces of film together. In the first place, you do not join the cellulose side of one piece of film to the emulsion side of the other, as usual. For a normal film splice you scrape the emulsion side of one of the two pieces of film, and then after applying film cement, bring the cell side of another piece of film in contact with the wet cement. When the process has been completed both pieces of film are the same way round—emulsion up in the splicer. When splicing spacing to magnetic, however, the principle is different. Here it is best to join cellulose to cellulose: the shiny side of the soundtrack should be brought in contact with the shiny side of the spacing: you do not even need to scrape the splice—just apply cement, or if you are splicing with tape apply the tape in the normal manner. The reason for making this kind of splice is a good one. Magnetic soundheads are tough pieces of equipment and they tend to scrape the emulsion off white spacing and clog themselves up, thus impairing the quality of sound reproduction. The cellulose side of spacing is harder than the emulsion side and is therefore not damaged in the same manner. The spacing can therefore pass over the head without clogging it and the soundhead will thus be able to reproduce the magnetic sound recorded on the track which is inter-cut with spacing in the best way possible. It is a small point, but one well worth remembering. When splicing magnetic to spacing splice cellulose to cellulose. When joining magnetic to magnetic splice in the normal manner.

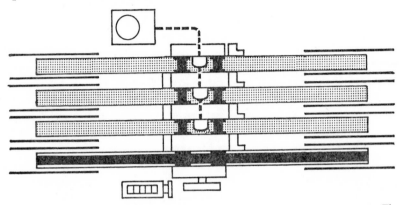

The synchroniser used for laying soundtracks. At the bottom is a footage counter. The picture runs through the nearest track to it. In the three adjacent tacks run separate magnetic tracks. Under each of these tracks is a magnetic soundhead, connected to an amplifier at the back of the sync. bench.

Laying Sound Effects

For laying some of the sound effects two pieces of equipment are essential—the editing machine and the synchroniser. First of all you run through the print on the editing machine to mark the exact spot where each effect is required. Draw a cross for each footstep at the point where the foot actually touches the ground. Mark a cross where a car door is opened and where it actually bangs closed. Indicate the point where a teacup touches the table—in fact, mark as many sync. points where effects are needed as you possibly can. Then remove the film from the editing machine and place it in the synchroniser. In one track you will need a roll of spacing. Mark a start mark on it level with the start mark on the picture and wind on to the first mark on your print. A glance at the print reminds you that it is a car door opening. Find the effect in the can and run it on the editing machine. Mark the exact frame where the effect starts and finishes. Now you can return to the synchroniser and

109

mark the spacing at a point level with the place on the print at which you have indicated the effect. Now you can join the mark on the spacing to the mark indicating the start of the effect on the coiled magnetic soundtrack. At the other end of the effect you can again splice on white spacing, taking care to splice it the right way round, cellulose to cellulose. You can now wind the film through the synchroniser. If you have spliced on the right point the magnetic stock should come opposite the mark on your cutting print. If it does, you can wind down to the next mark, where the car door closes. Here again you need to mark the spacing before selecting the effect and slotting it in in the same manner. This is the procedure for laying all spot effects. When you have reached the end take the film and the reel of magnetic track, intercut with spacing, out of the synchroniser and rewind them.

The next step is to check them on the editing machine. You will probably find a few of the effects need moving one or two frames one way or the other. Make the necessary adjustments. When you are sure all is right you can identify the start of the reel with the title of the film and the words *Effect 1*, or *Fx 1* as it is usually abbreviated. Now you can again turn your attention to the action.

So far, you have laid a commentary track and a track of footsteps, car doors and other spot effects. This is a good start but is by no means a detailed soundtrack. You must wind through and build up the rest of it. The editing machine will be most useful for this part of the work.

Many of the sound effects you still need are not *spot* effects. They last longer than the few seconds required for a footstep or for a door bang. For a few of these sounds you may be able to use loops. The remainder will form the basis of your other effects soundtracks. Let us look at the composition of these different tracks in terms of a definite situation.

Planning Effects—an Example

Imagine we have a dock scene where crates of materials are being loaded on to a ship by a crane. The crates are being moved into position by a fork-lift truck which puts them down at a point from which a crane picks them up and carries them away to the ship's hold. The script calls for several shots.

The first shot is a long one showing the whole of the ship and making the fork-lift truck very small and insignificant. The script points out that the field of view tightens as the camera concentrates

110

on the centre of the ship and the fork-lift truck standing alongside it. In the second shot, the fork-lift truck alone features. It lifts a pile of crates into position. The third shot is a wider view. It shows the overhead crane coming down to lift up the crates and carry them out of shot. We then go back to the fork-lift truck which is reloading. What does this mean in the terms of soundtracks?

The script also shows that there is no dialogue or commentary. The scene depends only on authentic sounds for its effectiveness. A background docks atmosphere loop will do much to create the atmosphere of the surroundings. Distant cranes, the sea, possibly a train shunting waggons far away, would be suitable material. This is a start. Now for the other effects.

On the first shot, both the crane and the fork-lift truck are very insignificant, but they should both be audible. In the course of the shot, the camera tightens the angle of vision to make them more obvious. They must be audible, for the sound mixer will want to fade up the sounds as the camera moves in to a closer view. You should therefore lay on one track the effect of a fork-lift truck and on the other the noise of the crane. Make sure you match the truck exactly to the action you are watching. Where the fork-lift truck moves off have the appropriate sound, and make sure the effect finishes when the truck has stopped moving. Likewise, watch the movements of the crane.

In the second shot we can only see the fork-lift truck. Obviously the audience will expect to hear the noise it is making, but possibly subconsciously they will also want to continue to hear the crane in the background. If the crane cuts out at the end of the previous shot they will think it has ceased to work. Carry the sound through.

On the first track you should have the fork-lift truck. On the second the crane, and on the third the noise of the crates being lowered to the dockside. A background loop will fill in the details. The third shot features the crane. This time you will need to carry the sound of the fork-lift truck through, even though it is not visible. When all the tracks are mixed together you will be surprised to find how authentic they sound.

Sound Cutting

Because the action in a scene comes to an end, you do not necessarily have to end the sound associated with it. Indeed, with skill and imagination one sound can be used to lead into a scene or to help smooth the transition from one scene to another. It is always wise to allow more sound than you actually need, for the sound mixer will be able to lose the part you do not want and a good overlap at the beginning and end of each effect may be useful. This does not, of course, apply where you are cutting from a scene filmed at one location to one shot somewhere entirely different. Then, cut the track, unless you wish to mix the outgoing and incoming sounds together.

Some sounds need to be eased in and out. If you are cutting from a scene of the interior of an airport departure lounge to a shot of a jet 'plane taxiing out to the runway, a straight cut from the gentle hubbub of the interior to the deafening roar of the jet might be distracting. In the normal course of events it is probably better to lay one of the effects on one track, carrying it on for several feet past the cut in the picture, and the other sound on another, bringing it in several feet before the change of scene. The sound mixer can then ease one out and the other in. Done quickly the effect will be entirely satisfactory and the abrupt effect of a straight cut will be avoided. This is a general rule, and, as with all rules, there are exceptions. If you are cutting a dramatic sequence showing someone racing through the airport reception hall, intercut with shots of the gangway being removed from a 'plane on the runway, you might well enhance the drama of the situation by cutting from one sound effect to the other. The straight cut would be more dramatic and would emphasise the difference in location.

Carrying Over Sound

The need to carry effects on when the subject of their origin does not appear on the screen is not always appreciated by inexperienced film makers. Sometimes you will see a film made by someone who thinks the audience only wants to hear what it can see. Consequently when a bus comes into the shot the soundtrack is suddenly filled with the noise of its engine. The moment it passes out of shot, the sound cuts off sharply. The overall effect is very unrealistic. The correct course to take is to find out where the bus comes into the shot and then run back a few feet. Start laying the noise of the bus several feet before it enters the picture. When it goes out of shot, carry the sound on for a few feet past the cut. When you make out cue sheets for dubbing specify the point where the mixer too should start fading up the effect and the place where it should be at full volume. The sound will then come and go smoothly just as it would if you stood in the street shown in the picture and listened to a bus going by.

112

Laying Music Tracks

In most films where music is used it is required only as a background. It should never be used to replace sound effects. Some film makers are lazy and feel that if they lay a few pieces of music over the scenes they need not be bothered with sound effects. They lose many opportunities, for sound effects are excellent on their own, but can also do much to augment music when heard behind it.

When you lay music, find out first of all where you want it to begin and to end. If you know where you want the end to be, wind the picture on to that point on the editing machine or in a synchroniser. Put the end of the music track you want to use opposite, at point where you wish it to end on the picture. Now wind back and listen to it. See if it fits well and if it comes in at the right place. If it doesn't, see if it can be faded up later without coming in at an unsuitable place.

Making Short Music Longer

Sometimes you find the music chosen is too short for the scene. If you are lucky you may be able to join two pieces of the music together in a manner which will not be detected by anyone but the composer. More probably you will find such a cut very noticeable. If so you must record the piece of music you want to use twice. Lay the start of the first recording at the point where you want it to start. Then proceed to the point the music section should end. On another track lay the other music recording back from the point at which you wish the sound to finish. Somewhere the two recordings will overlap. Now, if you lay the music skilfully enough, you may sometimes be able to mix from one track to the other in the course of the music. Certain kinds of music are more suitable than others. Percussion pieces are favourites for this kind of work. If you cannot mix across in an unnoticeable fashion, you will have to fade out the first piece and fade in the second. Pick a point where the fade out and fade in can be covered by sound effects and no one will ever notice. The audience will only be aware that the music comes in at a good point and goes out at a good one. The sound effects, if skilfully chosen and laid, will disguise the transition from one recording to another.

Dubbing Theatre Equipment

The work of combining the soundtracks on one piece of magnetic film can proceed once all the separate tracks have been laid. The

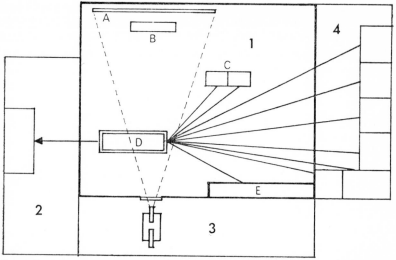

Room 1: soundproofed theatre. (A) Screen. (B) Footage counter. (C) Gramophone turntables. (D) Mixing console manned by dubbing mixer. (E) Commentary box. Room 2: sound recording room, containing recording equipment. Room 3: projection box, containing projector locked in sync. with recorder and reproducers. Room 4: sound reproduction room, containing series of sound reproducers.

dubbing theatre equipment in its simplest form consists of a projector which is locked in synchronisation with a number of 16 and 35 mm. sound-reproducing machines and one recorder. All the machines run at the same speed. The sound output of the reproducers is fed through a console containing numerous controls designed to alter the quality of each individual soundtrack as required. The console also contains a series of volume controls which make it possible to fade each track in and out or mix from one to the other as and when required. The whole operation is controlled by a sound mixer who sits at the console, watching the projected picture of your cutting copy on a screen in front of him. Underneath the screen is a footage counter. As the film moves on, the footage counter records its progress. In front of him, the mixer also has a detailed cue sheet. It tells him everything he needs to know about the film he is mixing. The sheet has been prepared in the course of editing. What does it show and how is it prepared?

Preparing a Dubbing Cue Sheet

The main purpose of a cue sheet is to tell the mixer exactly what is on each soundtrack and to specify the point at which each sound

114

starts and ends. You must also specify *how* you want it to start and end. Do you want it faded in or out, or mixed to another track or just left to cut out as you have laid it? The cue sheet can be prepared either on a synchroniser by running the action with all of the tracks, or on an editing machine by running the action several times with each different track.

Before you start, zero the footage counter on the equipment you are using when the first picture on the start of the film first begins. This is the starting point of your film footage. Always measure from the first frame of picture (unless sound precedes it) and not from the leader or spacing on the very beginning.

On page 117 you will find a specimen cue sheet for a normal type of documentary. The sheets have a standard form—the one illustrated is a vertical one, but some sound mixers prefer to use horizontal sheets. Whatever the format, the basic information contained on the form is standard practice. This particular cue sheet is for reel one of a film I produced on the work of artist John Piper. At the top of the sheet you should always write the title, the production company and the reel number.

The cue sheet is divided into several columns. The exact number of columns will depend on the number of soundtracks you have prepared. Each soundtrack must have its own column and the action must also have a column of its own. Additionally, columns must be found for the background loops you intend to use. On the cue sheet for *John Piper* you will see we are using four 16 mm. tracks and four loops. The left-hand column is devoted to the action. The first of the soundtracks consists only of commentary. The others are built up of a mixture of music and effects. You should never put commentary on more than one track and, where possible, it is not a bad idea to keep music on a track by itself.

Cued Sound Transitions

There are three main ways of putting two soundtracks together. You can cut from one to the other, you can fade one out and fade in the other, or you can mix the two sounds together, gradually losing one and at the same time increasing the volume of the other. Each of these ways has to be specified on a cue sheet—you have to let the mixer see at a glance exactly what you want him to do. He must know where each sound must come in, and how you want it intro-duced. He must also know what track it is on and where you want it faded out or boosted. He must know if you want the track reproduced at full volume or held low for a period and then brought up. The cue sheet must tell him all this, and specify the appropriate footage. He can then see the footage on the counter under the screen on which your cutting copy is projected. By referring to the cue sheet he can find out exactly what you want him to do at every given point. Let us now look at the *Piper* cue sheet in greater detail.

Mixing from the Cue Sheet

The film starts with an atmosphere loop—a general background which is faded in at 0 feet and has reached full volume by 1 ft. This loop is noted as track five on the cue sheet. The fade-in sign is simply a large inverted letter V. The narrowest point marks the start and the widest point the finish of the fade in. An upright V marks a fade out—full volume at the widest point, fading to nothing where the two sides meet.

If you want to mix from one track to another, you simply fade out one and at the same point fade in another. This kind of mix from one track to another is known as a cross mix. If you are not mixing to the track in the adjacent column on the cue sheet, it is worth putting a small dotted line across from one track to the other to remind the mixer that two operations have to be performed at that particular point. A straight line drawn horizontally across the track simply marks a cut. At 11 ft therefore the commentary cuts in on the Piper film cue sheet. It cuts out at 47 ft where, on track two, music cuts in. The atmosphere loop continues throughout. Track two has to be faded out with a fade starting at 79 ft and ending at 81 ft. Commentary cuts in on track one at 80 ft and out at 92 ft where music again replaces it on track two. At 137 ft there is a cross mix from tracks five to six. The atmosphere loop is gradually changed for a loop of countryside effects. A war sequence begins at 291 ft. It is built up on several different tracks all of which are, on several occasions, open at the same time. The battle begins with gunfire, on track three at 291 ft. This cross mixes at 310 ft to track two where Hitler's voice takes over. This is augmented by a series of 'planes which are faded up at 331 ft, to reach full volume by 334 ft. Hitler's voice starts to fade out one foot earlier but does not disappear completely until 339 ft. At the same time as the Hitler speech, on track four a crowd chanting, "Sieg Heil!" is faded up at 324 ft and cross mixed out to track three (the 'planes) at 334 ft. The main 'plane noises continue on track three but at 347 ft we have a more detailed shot which includes some 'planes taking off. These effects have been

Example of a dubbing cue sheet for a documentary film, using a vertical layout.

laid in the synchroniser to cut in at 347 ft and cut out at 370 ft, on track two. At 351 ft there is another prominent 'plane in shot and sound for this has been laid at 351 ft on track four. At this point

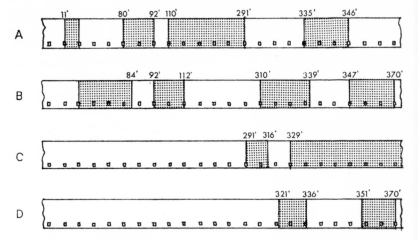

Composition of soundtracks for *John Piper—A Film Portrait*. (See also dubbing cue sheet.) Note particularly how tracks are cut in before fades are needed. Fades and dissolves on cue sheet appear as cuts on the actual tracks, though the cuts are always overlapping the required footages. Fading and mixing are done in the dubbing process, but tracks must be suitably overlapped beforehand.

tracks two, three and four are all open. And so it goes on until the end of the reel.

At the foot of the page is marked the end footage of the reel so that the mixer knows how much stock to use for recording the final mixed recording. The recording he makes is your final mix master track. From it, you will be able to produce either magnetic soundtracks of comparable quality or materials for printing of prints with married optical sound (also known as composite or combined prints).

Sometimes the sound mixer will not want to mix all your soundtracks at once. Perhaps, in the case of a major production, there are not enough reproducing soundheads to cope with all the tracks you want to contribute to the finished final mix. Possibly too many things are happening at a particular point of the film. In cases like this, the mixer will arrange to make a premix. This simply means that he will mix some of the tracks together first and then reproduce the partially mixed recording with the remaining tracks, mixing all together.

It is often best to premix all music and effects recordings before adding commentary. If you are planning to make foreign language versions of the film, this is of course essential, for a separate music and effects track (known as an M. and E.) is vital for language dubbing. It should be free of everything but synchronised dialogue, music and effects. Synchronised dialogue, not commentary

118

spoken out of view of the camera, should always be preserved on an M. and E.

Before you take your film into a dubbing theatre, check again that everything really *is* ready for the dub. Have you clearly marked the reel number and the track number on the head of each reel. If you turn up with a reel of picture and five unidentified reels of magnetic track you will waste a great deal of time finding out which are the tracks referred to in your cue sheets. Time in a dubbing theatre can be expensive. Above all, come with everything you need. Nothing is more frustrating than sitting round waiting for one loop or page of a cue sheet which you have accidentally forgotten to bring along. A sound mixer's enthusiasm to mix any picture can easily disappear!

Effects Done in Dubbing

Sometimes you may find you have to dub a film in a hurry. Having worked for a number of years in television I know in how much of a rush some films have to be prepared. You sometimes have only a couple of hours to put together five or ten minutes of film, dub it and have it ready for showing. On occasions like this, it may be impossible to lay all the soundtracks you require. You may be able to use gramophone discs to help you out for a versatile gramophone operator can often drop on sound effects recordings at a precise footage, although he too will want to be cued. Loops, too, may help in an emergency. Many effects can be done "live to picture" in the dubbing theatre, although this method should only be used by people with experience. Footsteps and other spot effects can often be reproduced quite satisfactorily in front of a microphone in the dubbing theatre although take care to match the perspective and acoustics of the actual picture being projected. Run through the cutting copy carefully beforehand. Note the footages at which effects are required and the precise nature of the effects. Get the "props" you will need together and have a rehearsal with the picture. If you are doing footsteps note carefully the type of surface people are walking on. Wood and stone are really quite easy. A few boards nailed together are adequate for mocking up floorboard effects and flagstones are suitable for any concrete surface. Sand is another easy effect to recreate. It is really easiest to put a small amount of sand in a sack and dampen it slightly. Fold over the top of the sack so that onne of the sand is actually visible, and make the footsteps required by prodding the sack with your fingers. If the movement is sharp and

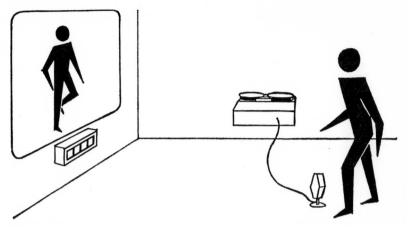

When adding sound effects to picture in a dubbing theatre, the effects man watches a screen and the footage counter underneath it and repeats the required actions, which are recorded on a recorder running in synchronism with the projected picture.

clear-cut it will sound exactly like footsteps on sand or on snow but be careful to match the exact movements of people on the screen.

Most spot effects are far better recorded in advance of dubbing and laid on one of your soundtracks. But when this is impossible, cigarette lighters, glass clinks and ordinary clothes rustles can all be done quite satisfactorily in a dubbing theatre by experienced people. Do not underestimate the small points like clothes rustles—they all lend something to a scene and it is always a good idea to put in relevant detail.

Re-voicing Dialogue

Sometimes the voices of synchronised dialogue sequences will be unusable. Possibly they are recorded in the wrong language for the intended audience. Alternatively, they may have just been badly recorded and background noise may drown the voice of the person who is speaking. In cases like this you will have to re-voice the scenes in question. Either the actor appearing in the scene, or one with a voice which matches the physical characteristics of the person concerned, must first be brought to the dubbing theatre. He must be given details of the script. The film must be broken down beforehand into loops—the actual length of the loop will depend on the amount of dialogue in each scene and how much the actor can remember. About 20 ft of continuous dialogue is about as much as the average person can cope with on 16 mm. The loops consist

120

simply of extracts from the cutting copy which are joined end to end to run continuously. These loops are placed on a projector and synchronised with a loop of new magnetic stock. The original soundtrack is sometimes run simultaneously and fed through headphones to the actor who uses it as a guide track. When he hears the dialogue start on the guide track he will start talking, trying to match exactly the lip movements of the action projected in front of him. His performance will be recorded and re-recorded over and over again as the loops revolve, until the director is satisfied that the voice exactly matches the lip movement. He will then stop the recordings and the loop concerned will be edited into the final version. The next loop can then be dealt with in the same manner. This technique is known as post-synchronisation. It is full of pitfalls but extremely useful and I have deliberately described it here in its simplest form. When re-voicing the film always take care to match the acoustics of the scene in question. If in the scene an actor is talking at some distance from the camera, his voice must be lowered accordingly when the action is re-voiced. These details are small but important.

Recording Commentary-to-picture

On occasions you may be unable to pre-record your commentary and lay it as a separate soundtrack. You will then have to record the commentary to the picture in the dubbing theatre. Again your commentator will take his cue from footages. Let him know when he will have to do his part, and cue him in. You can do this from footages or by switching on a light in front of him when you want him to speak, or simply by tapping him on the shoulder when you want his line to begin. Before you shoot anything, make your commentator comfortable and put him at his ease. Let him rehearse and go through the script with you until he is quite sure of it. Put the script flat, preferably in sheets of protective plastic, where it will not rustle, and make sure the chair he is sitting on does not creak. If you take these simple precautions you will save time and money when you dub.

At the end of a dubbing session you will have your edited cutting copy and a final mix master recording of your soundtrack. For the first time all your soundtracks will be on one piece of perforated magnetic film.

E

9

OPTICALS AND TITLES

A DISSOLVE consists simply of fading out one scene and simultaneously fading in another from a precise point. In the middle of a dissolve one scene should be half faded out and the other half faded in, the exact amount being calculated in frames. It is, of course, perfectly possible to produce fade ins and outs in the camera. You simply open or close either the lens stops or a variable shutter at the pace required. A dissolve can also be produced in the camera. You note the exact point where you start to fade out the first scene. Then without re-exposing wind the film back to the centre point of your required dissolve and start to fade in the second exposure, making sure the overall length of the fade in does not exceed that of the fade out of the previous exposure. The two scenes will thus be partially superimposed and, if the work is done with care and precision, an acceptable dissolve should be produced. But this system of camera opticals does have very serious limitations—serious enough in fact to make it impracticable to the professional film maker.

The biggest problem of all is knowing where you want a dissolve to come. When a film is exposed, it is almost impossible to know exactly at which point you will want to mix from one scene to another. In the case of titles it is all reasonably simple. You know that the first title must last for one length of time, and the second one for another, and can time your dissolve accordingly. When you are shooting live action it is very much more difficult to predict the right time to move from one scene to the other. Until the film is edited you are quite unable to tell where the best point is. It is far better to leave the whole question of optical effects until you have an edited version of the picture. You can then arrange for a laboratory to produce the correct effects for you. At this stage, you will have the edited cutting copy to help you. You can run through it as many times as you please until you are absolutely certain where you want to dissolve, or to fade in or out. You then simply order the effect required.

Indicating Opticals

You must first of all mark the length of the effect on the cellulose side of the cutting copy with a wax pencil. There are accepted ways of marking up different kinds of opticals. For a dissolve you mark a line from one side of the picture at one end of the dissolve, to the opposite side of the picture in the centre of the dissolve (where you have spliced the two shots in the cutting copy) and then back again to the other side to end at the point at which the dissolve is required to end. A fade out is marked by placing a large letter V in the picture. The open part of the letter should start where the fade out is required to begin and the base of the letter should mark its end. For a fade in, the procedure is reversed. A wipe consists solely of one straight line crossing from one side of the picture to the other in the required direction. These signs are internationally understood and require no further explanation. Their presence will guide the negative cutter when he starts to match the master material to your cutting copy. There is a further point to be considered when ordering opticals. To understand this we must first look at how opticals are made.

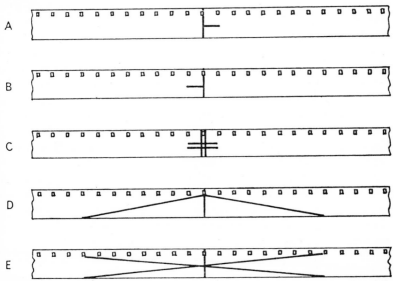

Signs used in editing procedure. (A) Cut. Lose right-hand portion. (B) Cut. Lose left-hand portion. (C) Carry through. Ignore cut. Do not match negative to it. (D) Dissolve (mix). (E) Fade-out. Fade-in.

Production of Opticals

We shall see later that there are two ways of matching negative to cutting copy. The negative when matched to the cutting print can be made up into two separate rolls, or can remain in one. If it remains in one, it is made to match the cutting copy precisely. Where there is a splice on the cutting copy there will be a splice on the negative and the scene will match scene frame for frame throughout the roll.

In the alternative method, the first scene will be on one roll of negative. If the second scene follows the first with a cut it may also be on the same roll, but if scene one *dissolves* to scene two, the second shot would be placed on a second roll of negative. The first roll would be carried on throughout the length of the second shot, only it would be built up with opaque spacing. At the next dissolve the incoming scene would be placed on the first reel and spacing would build up the second. This would be carried on to the end of the film, the negative being built up scene by scene to match the cutting copy on two separate rolls which, when printed together on the same roll of stock, would produce a single print identical in form to the edited cutting copy.

What is the advantage of dividing the negative into two separate rolls and why divide them where one scene dissolves into another? This kind of negative is known as an A & B roll and its composition and use is considered later.

At this point let us just consider why the reels are changed at dissolves and not necessarily at every scene change. To understand the answer to this problem we should really remember what has to be done to produce a dissolve if it is done in the camera. You fade out one picture, and fade in the other, overlapping the two actions. Now, obviously in a single roll of negative it is not possible to have two pieces of film physically overlapping each other. You must allow for the overlap by placing your negative on separate rolls.

On the first roll you place the outgoing shot. You leave the negative over length, allowing half as much spare film as the length of the actual optical. On the other negative reel you place the negative of the incoming exposure, this time overlapping the outgoing action by keeping an extra length of film at the beginning of the optical. Again the length required is half the length of the actual effect— for a 40-frame dissolve, 20 extra frames are required in each direction from the centre of the optical and so on. When the laboratory produce further prints from this negative they will start to fade out the outgoing shot on one roll of negative at one point. They will also fade in reel two and the required dissolve will thus be produced, on the print.

Opticals from Single Negative

We have seen how opticals can be produced from A & B rolls of negative, but this does not mean that optical effects cannot be produced in single reels of edited negative. This kind of optical is really just as commonplace although, in my opinion, not as good for the 16 mm. film. As you cannot overlap two pieces of film on a single roll of negative it is obvious that the effect must be produced on a single strip of film if it is to be cut into one reel of edited negative.

If you want opticals in a single negative you need to know how they should be ordered and how they are produced. The first point to remember is that, as you cannot overlap the two pieces of your original negative, you must make a duplicate in which the two actions are visually overlapped. To do this you first of all mark up your editing print in wax pencil in the way described above. You then look at the edge numbers alongside the two shots of film you wish to merge together. When you have noted the numbers you should locate the original pieces of negative in the cans which you have already carefully numbered. With great care cut these two shots out of the negative and splice them together placing some protective spacing on each end. Remove the whole shot from the negative and not just the part which appears in the edited picture.

Indicating Single Negative Opticals

When you have found the two pieces of original negative, send them to a laboratory with an optical order form. They will then produce the optical effect for you on a single piece of duplicate negative film. To do this they may use a special kind of camera, or they may simply produce a fine grain print of the two pieces of negative you have supplied, and make them up into A & B rolls before reprinting them on a duplicate negative stock. Optical order form books can be supplied by any laboratory. They are easy forms to complete and ask you merely to give details of the markings you have already placed on your cutting copy. They will ask you to specify the edge number at which you want the dissolve to begin and the points where you wish its centre and end to be. Also at which point you want the duplicate negative the laboratory will produce to start.

Always start the duplicate at the beginning of the shot. When you mark the beginning, middle and end of the dissolve or fade you may perhaps find that the point you wish to mark does not exactly coincide with a particular edge number. Perhaps one edge number covers several frames. How then do you specify the exact frame you want to point out? Here again there is a standard formula.

A foot of 16 mm. film (40 frames). There is one key (edge) number in every foot of film

Look for the nearest edge number and pick one frame on which a definite part of the number appears. Perhaps the number of JH3245974. This is a long number and perhaps only the figures 74 are really clear enough to stand out without careful study. Write the whole number on your optical order form (or sheet as it is often called) and mark a box round the figures 74. You have now pinpointed one specific frame. Now if you look again at the piece of film you will find that on either side of the edge number you have listed, at 1-ft intervals, are two other numbers. One is JH3245973 and the other is JH3245975. From these you can gauge the film's direction. Now look again at the frame you have specified with a box. Where, in relation to that frame, is the start of the optical effect you require? Is it to the right or to the left? Is it nearer 3245973 or 3245975? Next of all count up the exact number of frames between the frame you have specified and the frame at which you want your effect to start, and write the number down. Now, note the direction. Is the start nearer the higher number than the one you first noted, or nearer that which is lower? If it is nearer the higher one you put a plus sign next to the number of frames you have just noted. If it is in the opposite direction, mark minus and you have then pinpointed the exact position where you want your optical to start. Follow the same procedure for the beginning, middle and end of your optical and you will be able to present the laboratory with detailed instructions.

When the laboratory have prepared a duplicate negative incorporating the optical effects you will be able to cut this single piece of film into your single reel of edited negative and the two pieces of the

126

original can be disregarded. As soon as they return your fades and dissolves, first of all check the material supplied to make sure it is exactly what you ordered. Check each frame to make sure the effect is what you want, and then cut the duplicate material containing the effect into your original edited master material. Now, on all future prints the same effects will be reproduced.

Preparing Titles

At about the same stage of editing as the ordering of opticals, you must start to prepare the main and end titles for the edited film. The amount of work involved will depend on the nature of the title required. If the cameraman has simply shot a title card on which an artist has drawn both a still picture and the appropriate titles, all you will have to do is to edit the exposures into the final version. Try not to jump them in—a fade is much smoother and more impressive and, at the end of the film it is always nicer to fade out rather than simply cut to nothing. If the cameraman was told how long each title needed to be he may have produced the fades for you. He may even have mixed from title to title. If he did not know exactly what was required, these refinements must be added in the course of editing.

Superimposed Titles

Sometimes you may want to superimpose a title over a moving background. This is not as difficult as it seems. You simply shoot your titles on a black background. (I always find white lettering by far the most suitable for superimposition even when the background is in colour.) Choose a film stock which can be developed to a very high contrast and instruct the laboratory accordingly. When the lettering master has been developed, ask the laboratory to make a high contrast print. You can now align this print in a synchroniser with the background material you want to use. Consider the lettering your A roll and the background your B roll. Edit them exactly to length and they can then be printed together to give a combined print of both lettering and background. For A & B roll masters this really presents no problem. You simply have the lettering on one roll and when it runs out you splice on opaque spacing. On the other roll you have the background which carries through in the normal A & B roll manner up to the first optical effect where the rolls are changed in the manner I have already described. For single roll negative, the procedure is almost exactly the same. The only difference is that, instead of printing from two rolls, one of lettering and one of background, every time a print is required, you will only print once. From that print the laboratory will produce suitable single strip duplicate master material which can be edited into your cut negative or colour master.

Last Minute Titles

Sometimes you will find that the whole question of titles is left until the editing stages. You may then have to find a cameraman capable of producing good quality titles, possibly at speed. Make sure that before he starts work he has all the details he will need. Tell him first of all the kind of stock the rest of the film has been photographed on. Tell him if you want the first title to cut in (or, as he will say, be "put up"), or would you like it faded in? If you require a fade, how long do you want it to be? Are you thinking of a mix to the second title? If so, at what point, and how long do you want the dissolve to be? Tell him exactly what the material is needed for, and what material he should provide. He must know if you want only the master material, or a cutting copy as well. He will also need to know if you are working on negative or reversal, for if he shoots on the wrong one you may well find all the lettering is upside down and you have to stand on end to read it!

10

MASTER TO SHOWPRINT

You now have two main tasks to carry out. The sound must be prepared for the production of further prints, and the cutting copy must be matched to the master material so that further copies can be made. The latter process is known as neg. cutting.

Negative Cutting

At this stage of production you will see why it is worth winding through your master material when it is first delivered from the laboratory and marking the appropriate edge numbers on the top of the cans. You now have to find a matching piece of either negative or colour master for every shot you have in your edited cutting copy. The first thing to do is to wind through the cutting copy on a flat rewind bench and make a list of the edge numbers of the shots you want to use. You can then turn from the cutting copy to the unedited negative or colour master. Find the lengths with the appropriate edge numbers and, with great care, cut them out and hang them in a suitably protective bin. You can now place the cutting copy on a film horse and in the first track of a synchroniser. Next to it in the second track insert a new leader or piece of spacing with a start mark level with the start mark on your cutting copy.

Now wind your cutting copy to the first scene. Look for the very first edge number and then find the matching piece of master material. Place the number on the master material in the synchroniser exactly opposite the number on the cutting copy. Now run back to the start of the scene on the cutting copy and mark the same point on the edge of the negative with a wax pencil. This point can now be spliced to your new leader or spacing. Wind through to the end of the first shot and check the last edge number. Mark the point at which the shot ends, and—allowing several frames for a splice to be made—cut the master material after the mark. Now you can repeat the action for the next shot. Find the appropriate piece of master material and match the edge numbers with those of the cutting copy. Run back to the start of the scene and mark it. This point can now be spliced to the end of the previous shot. In this way you can proceed until you have a complete reel of master material which exactly matches your edited cutting copy.

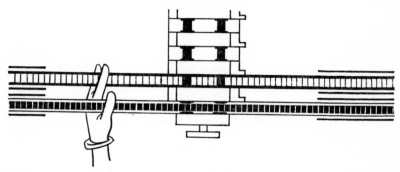

When negative cutting, the negative cutter runs the cutting copy in track one of the synchroniser and matches the negative to it in track two.

Sometimes you will find a scene is too short to have an edge number on it. In cases like this you will simply have to match the action on the cutting copy with that on the master material. On optical duplicate material, you will also find you do not have edge numbers which match the cutting copy—unless of course you have had a print of the opticals themselves, and have been far-sighted enough to match the action precisely.

I have spoken so far about single rolls of master material. Let us now consider two alternative systems, one of which I have already briefly mentioned, and the advantages they offer. These alternatives are A & B rolls and checkerboards.

We have already seen how, when editing master material to an edited cutting copy, the appropriate numbers are matched and the scenes spliced together on a single roll. Thus master matches the cutting copy in every detail. This procedure is known as negative cutting, and the system used is exactly the same if you are matching a negative or a reversal master to the cutting copy. For A & B rolls there are slight differences in the procedure for negative materials and reversal masters. To understand the differences, we must see how the A & B system works.

A & B Roll System

With the A & B system, the edited master in the case of a reversal film is matched to the cutting copy in exactly the same way as master material which is to be made up into a single roll. Only when the material is joined together does the difference between the A & B roll and the single roll become apparent. In the A & B system some shots are spliced not to the next shot, but to black spacing. The picture moves from one roll to another whenever a fade or a dissolve is needed. The overlap required, if any, is carried through on the outgoing roll and brought in before the centre point of the effect on the incoming one. When the two rolls of master are printed on one positive roll, in the case of a dissolve, one scene is faded out and another faded in at the same point. The scene which is to be faded out is put on roll A, and the incoming scene is spliced on the opposite roll, or vice versa. The two lengths of film must be overlapped so that the laboratory can fade out roll A and simultaneously fade in roll B. The exact length of the overlap required depends on the length of the effect required. Half the optical length is needed, so if you want a 60-frame dissolve you will need 30 frames of overlap.

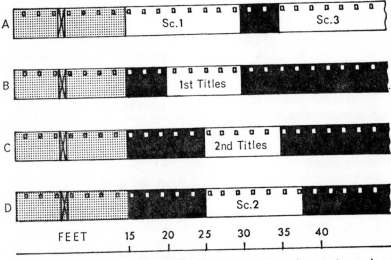

A and B assembly with extra C and D rolls to allow titles to be superimposed and background shots to mix from scene one to scene two. Background of shot I on A mixes to background 2 on D at $27\frac{1}{2}$ feet (note overlap). First title lettering cuts in on B at 20 feet and mixes to second on C at $27\frac{1}{2}$ feet (again note overlap). The second title cuts out at 35 feet and scene 2 on D mixes to scene 3 on A at 36 feet (again note overlap).

On the outgoing roll, after the end of the overlap, and on the incoming roll before the overlap is started, you have to splice black spacing.

Now, when the two rolls are printed together on to a single roll of positive stock, the laboratory will make the necessary fade out and fade in. Both these are at the same point but from different rolls. Now you have a dissolve.

A & B Roll Opticals

You only need an overlap in the case of a dissolve or a super-imposition. In the normal course of events you join the end of the first shot to the start of the second on the same roll. For A & B roll printing you only change from one roll to the other when a dissolve or wipe occurs. In a dissolve or wipe you need to move from one scene to another gradually and thus need to expose the two scenes together at the same point. As we have seen, you need an overlap to make this possible.

When you are fading in or fading out, however, you will not need any overlap for you are only concerned with the exposure of one scene at a time. Thus, it is unnecessary to move from one roll to the other.

Make a note of the footages of all optical effects and send a cue sheet to the laboratory when you order your prints. Tell them the footage and the effects and what is on each roll. For example, if you want a fade out at 516 feet, tell them which roll the outgoing and incoming scenes are on and how long, in frames, you want the fade out and fade in to be.

What is the advantage of this A & B system? The main benefit is that you are printing from the original material, not from a single piece of duplicate film which has been produced simply to incorporate the optical effect. As the original is being used, prints will be of better quality.

On the start of each roll of A & B roll assembly you must mark a start point and the roll number and film title. State which is roll A and which is roll B and, if the first scene starts on roll A build up B with black spacing. If you have a main title at the beginning which has to be superimposed over a moving background, in the A & B assembly you simply cut the background on one roll and the lettering on the other, building up the parts where there is no lettering with black spacing. When you come to the first optical, move from one roll to the other where it can be joined scene to scene. Carry on

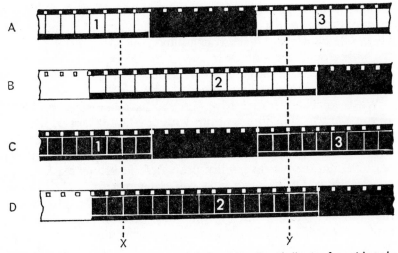

A

B

C

D

X   Y

Title assembly of master material using A B C and D rolls and allowing for a title to be superimposed over a moving background. Backgrounds and letterings mix from one to the other. A1, background of first title. B2, background of second title. A3, background of third title. C1, lettering of first title. D2, lettering of second title. C3, lettering of third title. X and Y are centres of dissolves (note the overlap).

until you reach the next optical where the materials can again be transferred from one roll to the other, overlapping if a dissolve is required.

Sometimes, perhaps, you may want to carry a title through a dissolve. In this case you place your dissolve on the A & B rolls in the normal manner, and make up an extra C roll for the lettering. Mark a suitable start mark on the head of roll C level with the starts for the other two rolls. Build up the track where not in use with spacing in the normal manner. There is no limit to the number of rolls you can add.

I have said that the roll not in use must be built up with *black* spacing. It is a good idea to do this right through an A & B roll assembly, but it is essential at points where titles are to be superimposed and scenes are to dissolve. If you think for a moment of the processes involved, the reason will become obvious. You are dealing with two simultaneous exposures. If you expose two scenes on top of each other, you must take care to see that you only get the effect you want.

If you splice white or clear spacing on to the end of the lettering you hope to superimpose, the printer light will flood through the clear film and fog the picture you are simultaneously exposing from another roll. If you have black spacing, it will stop unwanted light passing through the printer. Only the lettering, which must always be on a really black background, will shine through. Thus the background remains clear and correctly exposed. This is, of course, only true in the case of reversal master materials for which A & B rolls were originally designed.

When working with negative film you have one slight problem. If you want to superimpose titles you may find it best to make a duplicate negative incorporating the superimposition. This is because when you shoot white lettering on a black background on negative film the negative, when processed, will show black letters on clear film. On negative, you will remember, the tones of the original scene are reversed. If you print this on top of another scene the clear background will fog the other piece of film when it is exposed on top of it. So you must take precautionary measures. Make a fine grain print of the background and shoot the titles on negative film. Make a high contrast print of the titles and ask the laboratory to superimpose the high contrast print and the fine grain print and so make a negative that you can use for printing. This applies to superimposing negative titles. Most A & B roll printing methods can be applied equally well to negative or reversal, and A & B opticals are just as good as those on reversal film and equally easy to achieve.

Checkerboarding

There is one alternative to A & B printing—a system known af checkerboarding. It is basically the same as A & B, but instead os changing from one roll to the other only at opticals, the change is made at the end of each shot. If shot one starts on roll A, shot two will be on roll B. At the end of shot one black spacing is joined on roll A and the same spacing precedes shot two on roll B. This is carried through to the end of the film, putting each shot on a different roll and building up the blank spaces with black spacing. The small white flash which can betray 16 mm. negative splices will not appear. The checkerboard system eliminates it.

When you splice negative always use fresh cement and a really clean splicer. Make sure that the sync. bench is dust-free and do not use bent reels. You should always wear white linen gloves when you are handling negative and it is wise to mark only the edge of the film with your wax pencil. When you have finally matched all the scenes of your cutting copy to the master material,

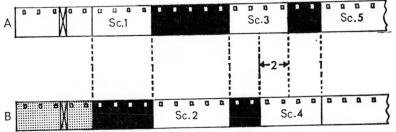

Checkerboard assembly. Both reels start with equal length leaders and level start marks. Scene 1 is on reel A, roll B simultaneously containing blank space. Scene 2 is on B—a straight cut from 1 on A. Scene 3 is on A—a level cut from 2 on B. Scene 3 on A dissolves to scene 4 on D (note the overlap). Scene 5 is a straight cut on reel A. In a checkerboard assembly, every shot is on a different roll.

you will have either a complete cut negative or an edited colour master from which further prints can be produced. But before you can make the final show print you must choose the kind of sound-track you want it to have.

Magnetic Showprint

There are two main kinds of print for general showing. One has an optical, photographic soundtrack, and the other has one which is recorded on a magnetic stripe on the edge of the print. On 16 mm. the quality of magnetic recordings usually exceeds that of an optical track, but, unfortunately, many projectors are unable to project magnetically striped prints. Let us look at the two different systems.

The magnetic soundtrack is easy to record but rather more difficult to check. It consists of a stripe of brown ferrous oxide coating on the side of the print on to which sound can be recorded. Your final mix master recording made in the dubbing theatre can be re-recorded on a magnetically striped print. Simply send the track with the print to a suitable transfer studio and ask them to transfer the master recording to the striped print. The process will not alter the recording on the master in any way. It will simply reproduce it on the striped print. But you must be sure that it is in correct synchronisation with the action. This is dictated by the layout of the sound film projector.

Sound Advance

The projector consists basically of a feed reel from which the film comes in the first place, a picture gate where the picture is actually projected, a soundhead where the sound is reproduced and a take-up reel. The soundhead and picture gate are in fact some distance apart, and that distance is very important. A print in synchronisation on one projector where the two are separated by a certain amount could be quite out of sync. on another where the distance is entirely different. With this in mind, international standards have been laid down. The distance between the picture gate and soundhead is known as the sound advance. On 16 mm. it is exactly 26 frames in the case of an optical soundtrack, and 28 frames in the case of a magnetic one. When your master recording is transferred to a striped print ready for projection, therefore, the sound must be advanced by 28 frames. The sound studio will advance the gate mark on the soundtrack by 28 frames before transferring the soundtrack on to the striped print. When the print is projected sound will be on the soundhead at the same time as the appropriate picture is in the picture gate 28 frames away and perfect synchronisation is thus assured.

The reason for this separation is that the movement of film through the picture gate is controlled by a claw, and is intermittent. Movement round the soundhead is smoothed out by a drum and is even and regular. Intermittent movement over a soundhead would produce terrible sound—it must be smooth and even and the standard amount of sound separation ensures this.

The magnetically striped print is usually of extremely good quality. It is a mistake to stripe prints which are full of splices, for if they are uneven it is often difficult to coat the surface of the film with an even stripe. It is always far better to make a new print, free from splices. This is particularly important to the solitary worker who likes to shoot his own film and edit the master material direct. He then sends his edited master away to be striped and records on the stripe. He would do far better to make a cutting print from his edited master. He can then edit that and, when it is ready, match the master to it. From the edited master he can produce a new, clean print without splices. If that is striped, he will achieve far better results than if he stripes his cutting copy.

Optical Tracks

The alternative system is the optical soundtrack. It is far more widely used chiefly because it is an older system and people are used to it. It is also much easier to check an optical soundtrack—the modulations are visible and faults can often be seen by those experienced enough to know what to look for. I am not, however, recommending optical recordings. They are a necessary evil. As I have mentioned before, optical soundtracks are produced by a photographic process. The optical track has to be printed and developed in the normal manner. A negative must first be produced and it can be made from your final mix master magnetic recording. How do you arrange for this negative to be made and prepare it and the picture for printing?

Before you do anything, mark an audibly recognisable point on the master magnetic recording. The accepted way to do this is to replace one frame of the leader with a frame of 1000-cycle tone,

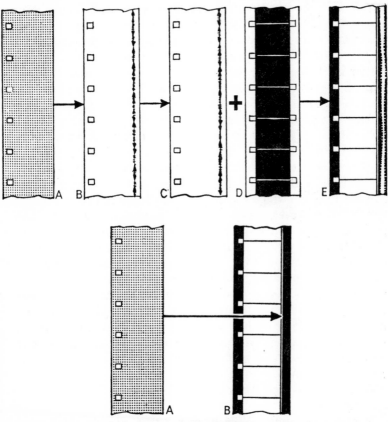

Stages of making a combined optical sound print (*above*). The master magnetic (A) is re-recorded on optical sound negative (B) which is then printed together with the picture negative (C and D) on positive stock to make a combined print (E). Stages of making a striped sound print (*below*). Re-record (transfer) master magnetic (A) to striped print (B).

which, when played, will reproduce as a "plop" or "bleep". Note exactly where you put this sync. tone, then send your magnetic track away for sound transfer. Ask the transfer suite to transfer it to optical sound negative, making sure you tell them the gauge of the track required, 16 mm. for 16 mm. printing and 35 mm. for 35 mm. prints. Tell them, too, the kind of negative you will be using to print the picture. The kind of track they produce must be the same type with the emulsion in the same position. Ask them to produce an optical sound negative but, if you are going to make married (combined) prints, do not ask for a print of the soundtrack alone. They will transfer the magnetic sound to optical negative and develop it and return it to you.

You are now faced with a reel of squiggly modulations. Somehow you have to synchronise it with your picture negative before you can produce married sound prints of picture and sound together. At this point, you must again place the edited negative or colour master in the film horse and synchroniser. Now look at the soundtrack. Somewhere near the beginning will be the plop of the frame of 1000-cycle tone which you attached to the leader. It will be easy to find—one frame of closely spaced lines which are bigger in the middle than they are on either side. Now remember where you put this frame on the leader of the magnetic. Place the recorded plop on the negative opposite the same point on the picture leader. Your sound is now in level synchronisation with the picture—exactly like the magnetic track recorded in the dubbing theatre. You will remember, however, that when the print you are about to order is projected on a sound projector, the sound needs to be farther ahead than the picture—26 frames ahead in the case of a 16 mm. married optical print. You must, therefore, pull the plop on the optical sound negative up 26 frames and then replace it in the synchroniser. It should now occur 26 frames before the point at which you attached a frame of tone to the leader of the master magnetic recording. When you are satisfied that this is the case, wind back to the very beginning of the reel and splice some spacing on to both picture and sound negative. Mark a large start mark on both, level with each other and write in clear letters the words "16 mm. print, sync. Start". After this splice on more protective spacing.

It may seem unnecessary to mark sync. at both the beginning and end of the negatives, but it is not. Some laboratories print the picture from the beginning of the roll to the end and then print the track in the opposite direction. It is also extremely important to mark the exact nature of the sound separation on both sound and picture near the appropriate start marks. If a start mark alone is put on without explanation, someone may well assume the two pieces of film are supplied in level synchronisation and pull up the sound a further 26 frames.

For 35 mm. printing the procedure is almost exactly the same, only the distance of separation differs. The 35 mm. sound is advanced 20 frames. This does not of course apply when 35 mm. pictures are reduction printed with a 16 mm. soundtrack. As the film is going to be shown on a 16 mm. projector, the advance must be 26 frames. The projector which will show the finished product dictates the sound advance required and for 16 mm. prints with optical soundtracks, 26 frames is the standard.

Ordering Prints

Now you must order your first print. It is always a good idea to ask the laboratory to clean the material they will use to make the print. Tell them too what you are sending. They will want to know if it is negative or reversal. They should be told if it is in level sync. or printing sync., and colour or black and white. Again, tell them exactly what you require. How many prints, and what kind of prints are you in need of?

If you are ordering the first print of a new film do not expect results overnight, particularly if it is in colour. All new films have to be carefully graded. Each light change must be worked out to ensure that every scene matches the one which precedes it. A detailed shot list can be helpful, particularly where the film contains night scenes. Sometimes the cutting copy can also be useful if there are a number of complicated opticals.

Checking the Prints

The laboratory will eventually produce your first married sound print. You will sit down and look at it with a critical eye. It is a very pleasant feeling seeing the first colour print of a film you have had to edit in black and white, though it can be rather a nightmare. You will be seeing the results of many weeks of work, but your own work is not quite finished when the first print is delivered. In checking it you must know exactly what to look for. Is it scratched? Is it in sync.? These are only two of a number of questions you must ask yourself.

Scratches are amongst the most common faults on both prints and negatives. Generally speaking, print scratches are black, though this can also apply to some scratches on negative, particularly those which have been caused in the camera. If you suspect your print is scratched, stop the projector and have a look at the print under a light.

You can usually see a scratch if it is on the print itself. If it is on the cellulose side you may be able to get it polished or waxed out but if it is on the emulsion side, there is little you can do unless you are checking a new print when you can, of course, send it straight back to the laboratory. On library material it is quite possible that a scratch may be in the original material. Nothing you can do to your copy will improve it. The same applies on duplicate negatives and negatives made from colour masters and reversal materials. If the scratch is not on the print you are looking at, you will have to check back each stage until you find it, if you wish to remedy the fault.

Negative scratches often appear white on the screen. The exceptions to this are, as I have mentioned, some camera scratches which may appear black. If the scratch has occurred before the original material was developed you can often find a small kink in the scratch at either the top, or the bottom. Alas, nothing can be done to remedy this kind of fault.

Other faults common on new prints are dirt and sparkle. Dirt on a print is usually black, and dirt on a negative prints as white sparkle. Dirt on the print itself can be cleaned off with a clean anti-static cloth immersed in carbon tetrachloride, but negative dirt must be removed before a print is made.

When you have checked you first print you are left with two main jobs. You must clear up the cutting-room and make a note of the copyright materials you have used in your final edited version. Let us consider copyright first.

As we have seen in an earlier chapter royalty payments for library material, and the use of copyright recordings of music and sound effects, are assessed on the amount of material used in the final edited version. Also the type of distribution the finished film is to have. Normally a fixed sum is charged for each thirty seconds of sound used from any particular recording. A film library will charge a similar set fee per foot of film. The exact charge will depend on the kind of audience the finished film is to be shown to. Thirty seconds of music or a few feet of library material used in a film made only for showing to the workers of one factory in the country where the film was produced will probably cost very little. The same amount of material used in a film for world cinema and television showing will cost very much more. These charges must be very carefully calculated. When the film is finished, run through the final soundtrack and note the exact footage of each piece of library film or commercial recording you have used. This, together with a copy of the dubbing cue sheet, if it lists in detail music tracks, should be sent to the film production office who will arrange for it to be relayed to the appropriate licensing authority.

Clearing up the Cutting-room

With this last editing task done, you can turn to tidying up the cutting-room. What a reward for a few months' work! And how untidy have you let it become?

Trims of your cutting copy can now be thrown away, and the soundtracks you used for dubbing can be reclaimed—but don't reclaim your new master recordings. Take out the spacing from the tracks you used in the dubbing theatre and join it up into rolls ready for use on some future production. Throw away short lengths of magnetic track unless you want to keep the sound effects for later use, and join up the longer pieces into rolls again ready for later use. Such reclaimed rolls can be used again when the recordings have been erased. With a number of splices they will not be suitable for recording master tracks but they may be quite adequate for recording effects which have to be laid for another production. It is probably worth keeping trims of your colour master or edited negative. If you have some material of general interest you may be able to sell it to a library as a stock shot. But I stress the material must be of general interest. Shots of your works foreman having tea, which the cameraman enjoyed shooting but which you never used, will not be welcomed by the library either!

Storage

You should carefully label and store all your master materials. Keep the master final mix and M. & E. tracks and the edited picture master. It is also worth keeping the cutting copy and the cue sheets in case you want to dub a foreign language version. Label them carefully with the name of the production company and its address on top so that the cans need never be lost. Write the full film title and the exact nature of the material on the label. It is useless just writing "magnetic", if it's your master track. Someone might think it is reclaim and use it again, then you'll be in trouble. State exactly what the material is. If it is a master track say so and then say exactly what kind of master track it is. A detailed label should tell you everything. "OPERATION MAGIC CARPET—MASTER MAG.", is inadequate. "OPERATION MAGIC CARPET, 16 MM. MASTER MAG. ENGLISH LANG. VERSION. CENTRE TRACK. ROLL 1 OF 1", is more useful. And if you're going to keep the cans in racks, it will help you if you first of all side-label the cans. Always keep film in a reasonable temperature. Avoid extremes of heat and cold and, above all, damp. From time to time it pays to rewind each roll through and check its condition. If you take simple precautions your film should last a lifetime.

When you have tidied the cutting-room your work is over. The results of all your efforts are now contained in a handful of cans. But when you see the finished product, you will not be disappointed if you have done the best you can do with the materials which were provided. The film has been edited and production is complete.

TECHNICAL TERMS

ACTION. When film is edited using separate soundtracks the picture to which the tracks are matched is often called simply "The Action".

BIG CLOSE-UP. (Abbr. B.C.U.) Shot taken very close to a subject, closer than would be necessary for a CLOSE UP—part of a human face, for example.

BLOW UP. The technique of producing a larger picture from a smaller gauge film. 35 mm. prints produced from 16 mm. materials are known as blow ups. 16 mm. prints made from 8 mm. are likewise blown up.

CLAPPER BOARD (*Slate*). Two pieces of board, hinged together in such a way that the two parts can be banged together at the start of a synchronised sound take. Scene and take number are written in chalk on the board so that the action can later be identified. The Film Editor matches the point where the two pieces of the board actually bang together, with the corresponding bang on the soundtrack and is thus able to synchronise sound and picture.

CLOSE UP. (Abbr. C.U.) Shot taken close to a subject and revealing detail. In the case of a human subject, a shot of the face only, the hands only, etc.

COLOUR MASTER or ORIGINAL. The name given to reversal colour materials exposed in the camera.

COMBINED PRINT. A print where soundtrack and action are printed together on the same piece of film stock. Also known as a married print.

COMMENTARY. Spoken words accompanying a film, the speaker usually remains unseen. Also NARRATION or OFF-SCREEN NARRATION.

CONTINUITY. The flow from one shot to another without breaks or discrepancies. Smoothness in the development of subject matter.

CONTRAST. The difference between lightest and darkest parts of a shot.

CORE. A plastic centre on which film is sometimes wound.

CROSS CUT. To alternate from one scene to another in the course of editing so that two or more subjects are presented in fragments, alternately.

CUE SHEETS (*Dubbing*). When all separate soundtracks have been matched to the action of a cutting copy, the footage at which each sound starts and ends is marked on a cue sheet. This guides the sound mixer as he mixes tracks.

CUT-AWAY. A shot of something other than the main action. A cut-away is inserted between shots of the main action, often to bridge a time lapse or to avoid a jump cut.

CUTTING BARREL. See FILM BIN.

CUTTING COPY or WORK PRINT. Often abbreviated to simply C/C, the cutting copy is the name given to the print used for editing purposes.

CUTTING-ROOM. The film editor's kingdom. It contains all the equipment needed for editing sound and picture.

DAILIES. See RUSHES.

DENSITY. Image blackness. A measure of the light transmitted by film.

DISSOLVE. An optical effect in which one scene gradually replaces another. In essence a fade-out and a fade-in are superimposed. Also known as a mix.

DOUBLE EIGHT. Unexposed 8 mm. film is often supplied in 16 mm. width with 8 mm. perforations. After exposing down one half-width of the film, the reels are removed, turned over and reinserted. Then the film is run through a second time exposing the remaining half-width. The 16 mm. material is then split to 8 mm. in the course of processing. The original 16 mm. stock, with 8 mm. perforations, is known as double eight.

DOUBLE EIGHT DUPLICATE COPY, or DOUBLE RANK COPY. There are many methods of multi-rank printing with 8 mm. For example 8 mm. prints can be made by a double rank negative on 16 mm. stock, by a triple or quad rank negative on 35 mm. stock. Also 8 mm. prints can be made by reduction from 16 mm. neg. (double perf.) stock or by split beam printing on 35 mm. stock.

DOUBLE SYSTEM. A system of sound recording used for shooting synchronised sound takes. Sound is recorded on separate magnetic film or $\frac{1}{4}''$ tape and not (as in the single system) on the actual film in the camera.

DUBBING. The name given to the various processes in re-recording a number of separate soundtracks to make one final mixed soundtrack. Also the name given to re-voicing a film in another language.

DUPE. Duplicate. A dupe neg. is a duplicate negative and not the original exposed in the camera. It is usually produced by printing a suitable positive stock on unexposed negative material.

DUPLICATING. Reversal materials, when printed on other reversal stocks, are often said to be duplicated. Where negative film is reproduced on positive stock the same process is known as printing.

EDGE NUMBERS. Also known as key numbers and sometimes as negative numbers. Edge numbers are to be found on the edge of film at intervals of 1 foot. The numbers originally occur on unexposed stock and are thus reproduced whenever the original material is printed. Used especially when the camera master (camera original) is matched to the edited cutting copy, and in the preparation of optical effects. Where edge numbers are missing or not legible, arbitrary numbers can be printed on originals and prints. This is known as "coding".

EDITING MACHINE. The term "Moviola", the trade name of a particular model, has now passed into general use to describe any editing machine.

EDITING RACK. A bar with pins on which clips of film are hung.

EDITORIAL CUT. See LEVEL CUT.

EFFECTS. Sound effects. FX for short.

EMULSION. The side of the film coated with light sensitive materials in the case of picture stock. The side of a magnetic track coated with ferrous oxide. Easily identified in either case as the least shiny of the two sides.

144

FADE-IN. Gradual emergence of a shot out of darkness.

FADE-OUT. A shot that gradually disappears into complete darkness.

FILM BIN. Large receptacle into which film is allowed to fall while assembling shots or when running film through a viewer or projector instead of using a take-up spool. In the U.S.A. film barrel or cutting barrel are the usual terms.

FINAL MIX. The final soundtrack, containing all music, dialogue, commentary and sound effects. This is the soundtrack the audience hears.

FINE GRAIN. Film stocks with extremely fine grain emulsions used for the intermediate stages in the course of producing duplicate materials.

FINE GRAIN POSITIVE, FINE GRAIN MASTER POSITIVE, or DUPLICATING PRINT. Intermediate fine grain or protection material normally indicated specifically by type, giving the number (e.g. EK-7255 or EK 7253).

FRAME. A single picture on a length of cinematograph film or the corresponding amount of a perforated magnetic soundtrack. The lines dividing a picture into frames horizontally are known as frame lines.

GRADING or TIMING. Estimating the amount of light that must be passed through the individual scenes in the matter of a film to produce the correct exposure in a print. This operation is usually done by eye. But linex strips or Hazeltine Liner (for colour).

INTER-NEGATIVE. A duplicate colour negative. In the U.S.A. refers primarily to a colour negative derived directly from a colour reversal original, while other negatives are known as "colour dupe negatives".

INTER-POSITIVE. A fine grain colour print used in the course of making duplicate colour negatives.

JUMP CUT. A cut which breaks the continuity by omitting an interval of time, revealing persons or objects in a different position in two adjacent shots.

LAYING SOUND. To place sound in its correct relationship with picture.

LEADER. A blank piece of film attached to the beginning of all reels of film. Contains a start mark and numbers at each footage down to 3 feet from the start of the first frame of picture. Similar leaders are also attached to all soundtracks. In the U.S. the term "projection leaders" is used. These are identified there as Academy or SMPTE leaders and further identified as Head or Tail leaders.

LEVEL CUT, STRAIGHT CUT or EDITORIAL CUT (U.S. terms). A cut where sound and picture are cut at the same point.

LEVEL SYNCHRONISATION. Where picture and soundtrack are kept in alignment. U.S. term Editorial Sync.

LIBRARY SHOT. Shot used in a film, but not taken specially for it; shot taken from a film or library source outside the actual unit producing a film.

LOOP. Short length of film joined at its ends to form an endless loop so that it can be projected repetitively, either to enable actors to fit words to lip movements or to enable sound effects to be fitted. In the case of soundtracks, a loop is frequently made up of continuous sounds such as crowd noises, wind, sea breakers, etc. This loop plays continuously and can be mixed in with the others at any time during a sound session.

M and E TRACK. A mixed music and effects track which is free of commentary. Essential if foreign language versions are required. M and E tracks should always contain all lip-sync. dialogue.

MAGNETIC. Magnetic film stock, usually perforated, for sound recording.

MAG. STRIPE. Magnetic coating on the side of film used for sound recording.

MARRIED PRINT. A print where sound and picture are combined on the same piece of film stock. U.S. terms "Composite Print" or "Combined Print".

MASTER. A camera master is the original camera material, also known by the term ORIGINAL particularly in the U.S.A. Master magnetic recording is the original sound recording.

MEDIUM SHOT. (Abbr. M.S.) Shot taken with the camera not so far away from the subject as for a LONG SHOT but not so close as for a CLOSE UP.

MIX. Another name for a dissolve.

MUTE. A picture negative or positive print without a soundtrack.

NEGATIVE. A piece of film where the tone values of the image are reversed. Black is white and white is black.

NEGATIVE CUTTER. The person who matches master and cutting copy.

NEGATIVE CUTTING. The matching of original negative (or colour master) to the edited cutting copy.

OPTICAL (*Effect*). Dissolves, fade-ins and outs, wipes and other special effects are known as opticals.

OPTICAL DUPE. Duplicate materials made in producing optical effects.

OPTICAL SOUNDTRACK. A photographic soundtrack, printed. Sound modulations are visible.

POSITIVE. Print.

POST SYNCHRONISATION. Recording sound to a picture after the picture has been shot.

RELEASE PRINT. Projection print of a finished film.

REVERSAL FILM. A type of filmstock which after exposure and processing produces a positive image instead of a negative.

RUSHES. Film that has just been exposed by a film camera. In the case of a print, a print of scenes exactly as they were shot in the camera without any cutting or editing having taken place. Also known as Dailies.

SHOW PRINT or RELEASE PRINT. Projection print of a finished film.

SLATE. See CLAPPER BOARD.

SOUND STRIPE. See MAGNETIC STRIPE.

SPACER or SPACING. See LEADER.

STOCK SHOT. See LIBRARY SHOT.

STRAIGHT CUT. See LEVEL CUT.

TRIMS. Unwanted portions of shots.

WAX PENCIL. A grease or wax pencil used for marking the edited work print. A yellow pencil may be used to indicate visual effects (such as fades, dissolves, etc.) and a red pencil to indicate recording or mixing effects.

WORK PRINT. Print used for editing purposes. It is usually an ungraded print taken from all or part of the camera original. Also CUTTING COPY.

146

FILM RUNNING TIMES AND FOOTAGES FOR 16 mm. FILM

(Calculated to the nearest I ft)

Running Time (mins)	Footage at 24 fps	Footage at 25 fps
1	36	37
2	72	75
3	108	112
4	144	150
5	180	187
6	216	225
7	252	262
8	288	300
9	324	337
10	360	375
15	540	563
20	720	750
25	900	938
30	1080	1126
35	1260	1313
40	1440	1500
45	1620	1687
50	1800	1876
55	1980	2063
60	2160	2250

Footage	Running Time (min/sec) at 24 fps	Running Time (min/sec) at 25 fps
1·16	0·2	0·1
2·16	0·3	0·3
3·16	0·5	0·4
4·16	0·6	0·6
5·16	0·8	0·8
6·16	0·10	0·9
7·16	0·12	0·11
8·16	0·13	0·12
9·16	0·15	0·14
10·16	0·17	0·16
25·16	0·42	0·40
50·16	1·23	1·20
75·16	2·5	2·0
100	2·47	2·40
150	4·10	4·0
200	5·33	5·20
250	6·57	6·40
300	8·20	8·0
350	9·43	9·20
400	11·7	10·40
450	12·30	12·0
500	13·53	13·20
550	15·16	14·40
600	16·39	16·0
650	18·2	17·20
700	19·25	18·40
750	20·48	20·0
800	22·11	21·20
850	23·34	22·40
900	24·57	24·0
950	26·20	25·20
1000	27·43	26·40
1500	41·36	40·0
1700	47·8	45·20
2000	55·26	53·20

INDEX

149

150

151